BILLY GRAHAM

Evangelistic Association

Always Good News.

Dear Friend,

I am pleased to send you this copy of *The Grace Controversy* by Dr. Michael Brown. Dr. Brown has written for *Decision* magazine and is the host of the talk radio show, "The Line of Fire," and the apologetics TV show, "Answering Your Toughest Questions."

In *The Grace Controversy*, Dr. Brown invites you to discover what God's Word says about the gift of grace. Using Scripture, he separates Biblical truth from popular misinformation and explores topics like legalism, the role of the law in the believer's life, and victory over sin. I pray that as you read this book, you'll be encouraged by the Bible's promise that, "*God is able to make every grace overflow to you, so that in every way, always having everything you need, you may excel in every good work*" (2 Corinthians 9:8, HCSB).

For more than 65 years, the Billy Graham Evangelistic Association has worked to take the Good News of Jesus Christ throughout the world by every effective means available, and I'm excited about what God will do in the years ahead.

We would appreciate knowing how our ministry has touched your life. May God richly bless you.

Sincerely,

Franklin Graham
President

If you would like to know more about our ministry, please contact us:

IN THE U.S.:
Billy Graham Evangelistic Association
1 Billy Graham Parkway
Charlotte, NC 28201-0001
BillyGraham.org
info@bgea.org
Toll-free: 1-877-247-2426

IN CANADA:
Billy Graham Evangelistic
   Association of Canada
20 Hopewell Way NE
Calgary, AB T3J 5H5
BillyGraham.ca
Toll-free: 1-888-393-0003

THE
GRACE
CONTROVERSY

MICHAEL L. BROWN, PhD

CHARISMA
HOUSE

This *Billy Graham Library Selection* special edition is published with permission from Charisma House.

A *Billy Graham Library Selection* designates materials that are appropriate for a well-rounded collection of quality Christian literature, including both classic and contemporary reading and reference materials.

This *Billy Graham Library Selection* special edition is published with permission from Charisma House.

THE GRACE CONTROVERSY
   by Michael L. Brown, PhD
Published by Charisma House
Charisma Media/Charisma House Book Group
600 Rinehart Road
Lake Mary, Florida 32746
www.charismahouse.com

Unless otherwise noted, all Scripture quotations are from the Modern English Version. Copyright © 2014 by Military Bible Association. Used by permission. All rights reserved.

All Scripture quotations marked CJB are from the Complete Jewish Bible. Copyright 1998 by David H. Stern. Published by Jewish New Testament Publications, Inc. All rights reserved. Used by permission.

Scripture quotations marked ESV are from the English Standard Version. Copyright © 2001 by Crossway Bibles, a division of Good News Publishers. Used by permission.

Cover design by Vincent Pirozzi
Design Director: Justin Evans

Visit the author's website at www.AskDrBrown.org.

Library of Congress Cataloging-in-Publication Data:
Names: Brown, Michael L., 1955- author
Title: The grace controversy / Michael L. Brown.
Description: First edition. | Lake Mary : Charisma
House, 2016. | Includes
    bibliographical references and index.
Identifiers: LCCN 2016006420| ISBN 9781629989198
(trade paper : alk. paper) |
    ISBN 9781629989204 (e-book)
Subjects: LCSH: Grace (Theology)
Classification: LCC BT761.3 .B748 2016 | DDC
234--dc23
LC record available at http://lccn.loc.gov/2016006420

While the author has made every effort to provide
accurate Internet addresses at the time of publication,
neither the publisher nor the author assumes any
responsibility for errors or for changes that occur after
publication.

First edition

16 17 18 19 20 — 9 8 7 6 5 4 3 2 1
Printed in the United States of America
    ISBN 978-1-59328-625-5 (BGEA edition)

CONTENTS

Introduction

AMAZING GRACE!

I T SEEMS LIKE every few decades a fresh wave of teaching on the subject of grace sweeps through the church. Often it brings a needed corrective, since it is very easy for believers to fall into a legalistic mind-set, almost forgetting what Jesus did for them on the cross. At other times the message goes too far, mixing dangerous error with glorious truth.

This is where we find ourselves today with what many are calling the "grace revolution." There is a wonderful emphasis on grace, but in many cases it is an exaggerated emphasis, one that goes beyond what the Scriptures say and even introduces serious error. I, along with other leaders, have called this modern, exaggerated message "hyper-grace," and I devoted an entire book to the subject titled *Hyper-Grace: Exposing the Dangers of the Modern Grace Message.*

The book was released in January 2014, and very quickly we began to receive requests from around the world, asking for the rights to translate the book as soon as possible. Last year I returned from a ministry trip to Europe with copies of *Hyper-Grace* in Italian and Dutch, and when I got home, there was a copy of the Finnish translation of the book on my desk.

This points to how widely this hyper-grace message has spread around the world and how urgent it is that we address its errors. Yet there is no denying that many have been helped by this same message, or at least by parts of it. How do we sort this out?

In *Hyper-Grace* I cited most of the main hyper-grace teachers—men whom, with rare exception, I consider brothers in the Lord, despite their exaggerated message—citing their actual words and getting into in-depth scriptural and theological discussion. Not surprisingly, the book was more than three hundred pages long, since I was eager to be fair to those I differed with and was even more eager to exalt biblical grace while correcting hyper-grace.

This book is an entirely new work, adapting very little content from the previous book and using a wholly different approach. (I also adapted some paragraphs from my 1999 book *Go and Sin No More: A Call to Holiness*.) The discussion here is much simpler; with the exception of one short quote, no hyper-grace teachers are cited; and I have written the book to answer twelve of the most common questions believers have after being exposed to the hyper-grace message (which I also refer to as the "modern grace" message).

As for the structure of this book, each chapter is complete in itself, but while the chapters can be read in any order, there is a logical progression, with the later chapters building on the earlier ones. So it is best to read this little book from beginning to end. But, to repeat, the chapters can with profit be read in any order, and I will always refer you back to an earlier chapter for more insights when relevant.

I also want to make a note about some of the terminology I use. In recent years I have increased the call for teachers, preachers, professors, and Bible translators to stop using the name "James" in place of "Jacob" in reference to Jesus's disciple (as the Greek uses Jacob throughout the New Testament).[1] So throughout this book I use Jacob with James in parentheses.

With this book my goal is to edify and strengthen and encourage, and my goal—really, God's goal—is to see people flourish in God's grace: biblical grace, glorious grace, amazing grace. When believers fully embrace it, they will have no need for the exaggerated and erroneous message of hyper-grace.

For those wanting more in-depth discussion of the themes in this book, I encourage you to get a copy of *Hyper-Grace* and work your way through the many endnotes and references. You can also visit my website, AskDrBrown.org, for many free, relevant resources, including audio, video, and written materials.

My prayer is that you will be established in God's grace as you read this book, and so I echo the doxology of Paul, "May the grace of the Lord Jesus Christ, and the love of God, and the fellowship of the Holy Spirit be with you all" (2 Cor. 13:14, NIV).

Chapter 1

IS GRACE A PERSON?

I've heard it said that grace is a person and His name is Jesus. Is that true?

OFTEN WHEN GIVING a definition of grace, modern teachers will say grace is a *person* rather than a *noun* and the name of that person is Jesus. It's a very catchy saying, but is it true? Grace certainly came through a person, but is grace itself a person?

Jesus was filled with grace and truth. He was the embodiment of God's grace. He was grace in action, dying to pay for our sins, rising from the dead to justify us, sending His Spirit to empower us, and always interceding for us in heaven. But grace is not Jesus. Grace is a noun, brought to us by a person whose name is Jesus. He brings grace to us and demonstrates grace to us. But in the Bible grace is not a person but a noun—a wonderful, glorious noun!

Let's look at some relevant verses that make this perfectly clear.

- "The Word became flesh and dwelt
  among us, and we saw His glory,
  the glory as the only Son of the
  Father, full of grace and truth"

(John 1:14). So we see that Jesus is full of grace and truth but is not grace Himself.

• "But we believe that through the grace of the Lord Jesus Christ we [the Jews] shall be saved, even as they [the Gentiles]" (Acts 15:11). Here Peter speaks of the grace of the Lord Jesus, which would make no sense at all if grace is a person and His name is Jesus.

Paul also speaks of "the gospel of the grace of God" (Acts 20:24), which makes no sense if grace is a person and not a noun. Of course, the message of God's grace is *all about Jesus*, but that is very different from saying that grace *is* Jesus.

Could it be that some people who say, "Grace is a person, and His name is Jesus," are avoiding giving a clear definition of grace? Really now, when you ask someone to define grace and you're given an answer like this, what has the person actually told you? Every true Christian believes in Jesus and loves and follows Him, so when teachers define grace by saying, "It's a person named Jesus," they haven't told us anything at all. What exactly do they mean?

Let's look at some more verses that speak about God's amazing grace.

Paul wrote, "But the free gift is not like the trespass. For if through the trespass of one man many died, then how much more has the grace of God and the free gift by the grace of the one Man, Jesus Christ, abounded to many" (Rom. 5:15). Paul again speaks of the grace of God and then the grace of that one man Jesus Christ, which is very different than saying grace is a person.

In keeping with that, Paul speaks of "the grace of our Lord Jesus Christ" five times in his letters (Rom. 16:20; 2 Cor. 8:9; Gal. 6:18; 1 Thess. 5:28; 2 Thess. 3:18). If grace is a person and His name is Jesus, what would these verses mean? Would Paul be speaking about the Jesus of our Lord Jesus Christ?

In Romans Paul wrote, "To all who are in Rome, beloved of God, called to be saints: Grace to you and peace from God our Father and the Lord Jesus Christ" (Rom. 1:7). Notice that peace and grace come *from* the Father and the Son, but neither peace nor grace *are* the Father and Son. See also his greeting to the Corinthians: "Grace to you and peace from God our Father and the Lord Jesus Christ" (1 Cor. 1:3).

So I think it should be pretty clear by now that grace is a noun, not a person. But, to repeat, it is a glorious noun, and it is all about Jesus, so let's focus on the grace that comes to us through Him.

MORE THAN UNMERITED FAVOR

Almost twenty-five years ago I did a serious study of the concept of grace in the Bible. I opened up my Hebrew and Greek concordances and examined every reference where the key words for "grace" occurred. Then I arranged them in different categories and prayerfully analyzed the usage. I was amazed by what I found, especially in the New Testament!

You see, grace is more than "unmerited favor" (although unmerited favor is nothing to snivel at). It is more than God's Riches At Christ's Expense (although that acronym sums up everything we will ever have or experience in God). God's grace is more than just a word or a concept, more than the manner in which God deals with us (as in, "I'm saved by grace, and everything I do is by grace"). It's more than that. It is His merciful, enabling help, His ongoing empowerment, His continued working on our behalf. It speaks of the Lord's past, present, and future action, expressing what Jesus *does* for us and not just what He *did* for us. As expressed by A. M. Hunter, "Grace means primarily the free, forgiving love of God in Christ to sinners and the operation of that love in the lives of Christians."[1]

Let me take a few minutes and explain this to you. Are you ready to do some study?

We'll begin with verses in which "grace" (*charis* in the Greek, which sounds like *car* plus *iss* in English) does mean unmerited favor. Here are some clear examples:

But we believe that through the grace of
the Lord Jesus Christ we shall be saved,
even as they. [In context, salvation by
grace is being contrasted with salvation
by works.]

—Acts 15:11

Therefore the promise comes through
faith, so that it might be by grace.

—Romans 4:16

I do not nullify the grace of God. For
if righteousness comes by the law, then
Christ died in vain.

—Galatians 2:21

In each of these verses you could substitute
"unmerited favor" for "grace," and the meaning
would be the same. So we can see that we're on
solid footing here.

It was this emphasis on grace that became a
foundation of the gospel message. (See John 1:17,
"For the law was given through Moses; grace and
truth came through Jesus Christ.") So the message became known as the gospel of grace, as the
following verses attest:

So Paul and Barnabas spent consider-
able time there, speaking boldly for the
Lord, who confirmed the message of his
grace by enabling them to perform signs
and wonders.
—ACTS 14:3, NIV

Nor do I count my life of value to myself,
so that I may joyfully finish my course
and the ministry which I have received
from the Lord Jesus, to testify to the
gospel of the grace of God.
—ACTS 20:24; SEE ALSO ACTS 20:32

How glorious is this gospel of grace! As filthy
as we were, as undeserving as we were, as dam-
nable and ungrateful as we were, Jesus died for
us. The Father set His love on us—even though
we were rank rebels—and adopted us as His very
own sons and daughters, actually making us *joint
heirs* of the universe with His Son. Hallelujah!
This is the most wonderful news that a mortal
ear could ever hear, and it expresses a goodness
beyond human comprehension. We had huge,
eternal debts that were damning our souls. Jesus,

who owed us nothing, paid them all. That's why Paul could write that we are "justified freely by His grace" (Rom 3:24). God can pronounce us "not guilty" because of what His own Son did.

This is the foundation of our spiritual lives, and it is the anchor for our souls. God accepted us because of what Jesus did, not because we stopped getting drunk or because we threw away our drugs or because we stopped sleeping around. It's actually the reverse: we stopped doing these sinful things because of what Jesus did for us, because He died in our place, because He took our shame and our guilt, because He paid the penalty for our sin, because He took what we deserved, canceling our debt when He hung on the cross.

The moment we put our trust in Him as Lord and Savior, our spiritual account was adjusted, and the Father looked at us and said, "Not guilty!" What's more, He said, "You are now righteous." And what's more than that, He said, "You are now My beloved child." That is the grace of God—from the prison of sin to the palace of the Savior, from a child of the devil to a child of the King, all because of the blood of Jesus.

That's why we can declare, like the popular Christian song of the 1970s, that we stand clean before our Lord, and not one blemish does He see. And that's why the hymn "Amazing Grace" has been one of the enduring classics of the church. Even the word *amazing* falls short of describing how incredible God's grace is. When we were utterly helpless, He helped us, and He continues to help us every day of our lives. That is the meaning of grace.

GRACE EMPOWERS

But here is the surprising news: the New Testament word *grace* does *not* fundamentally mean "unmerited favor." Its basic meaning does include favor (of any kind) along with kindness, but it also includes enablement and gifting, important concepts we often miss.

You see, God's grace not only *did* something amazing for us—forgiving us for all our sins—but His grace *continues to do* something amazing for us—empowering us to live for Him. In fact, there was nothing revolutionary in the New Testament concept of grace meaning "favor" or "gift." What was revolutionary was the degree of favor shown to us through the Cross and the ongoing effectiveness of that favor in our lives. Grace finishes what it starts.

Why is this so important to understand? It is because many believers know that God saved them by His grace and that He continues to deal with them based on His grace, but they don't know that His grace is *presently at work* in them. In other words, it's one thing to say, "All that I do, I do by the grace of God," meaning I don't deserve any credit or honor (which is true). It's another thing to say, "The grace of God worked mightily in me," meaning I was supernaturally helped by God to do His work.

Do you see the difference? It's one thing to say, "I come to God through His grace," meaning I have access to God through the blood of His Son (amen to that!). It's another thing to say, "I serve God daily through His grace," meaning I am enabled to do His will because He Himself is at work in me. There is a distinction here.

One believer says, "I'm not under the law; I'm under grace" (see Romans 6:14), taking it (wrongly) to mean, "God understands my sins and doesn't condemn me for them. He receives me just the same regardless of how I live." Another believer says, "I'm not under the law; I'm under grace," taking it (correctly) to mean, "Through grace I'm not only forgiven for my sins, but also I can now live above sin. Whereas the law could only point out my shortcomings, God's grace can transform my nature." That is the power of grace! (See chapter 6 for more on this.)

God's grace is comprehensive and complete. It saves and sanctifies, rescues and restores, transforming us from hell-bound sinners to holy-living saints. That's the grace of God! And just as it was the Lord's supernatural, infinite grace that saved us, it is His supernatural, infinite grace that keeps us. It is truly an ocean of grace that we experience in Jesus.

Look back and see how the Lord began to deal with you. It was all grace! You were a hopeless slave to sin, a rejected wretch, a captive to the will of the flesh. "But because of his great love for us, God, who is rich in mercy, made us alive with Christ even when we were dead in transgressions—it is by grace [*charis*] you have been saved" (Eph. 2:4–5, NIV). Who can fathom God's grace?

But that is only the beginning. His grace is with us this very hour, helping us, keeping us, empowering us. That's why we can "come with confidence to the throne of grace [*charis*], that we may obtain mercy and find grace [*charis*] to help in time of need" (Heb. 4:16). What encouraging words! For His children, God's throne is a place of help, mercy, and favor, and at that throne we find everything we need. Praise God for the stream of grace that flows from the throne of grace.

And yet there is more. We can also look ahead to future grace: "And God raised us up with Christ and seated us with him in the heavenly realms in Christ Jesus, in order that in the coming ages he might show the incomparable riches of his grace [*charis*], expressed in his kindness to us in Christ Jesus" (Eph. 2:6–7, NIV). In light of this—who can imagine what it will be like?—Peter urges us, "Set your hope fully on the grace [*charis*] that will be brought to you at the revelation of Jesus Christ" (1 Pet. 1:13, ESV). What a day that will be! Grace, more grace, and endless grace—that sums up our past, present, and future in Jesus. Do you realize what this means?

It means we can rest confidently in the goodness of our God, knowing that the same blood that washed us in the beginning continues to wash us in this hour, and that the same grace that helped us in the past continues to help us in the present. God favored us by setting His love on us, and He favors us by keeping His love on us.

How were we saved? By grace through faith. How are we kept? By grace through faith. What is our eternal hope? Grace through faith. Revel in it; rejoice in it; delight in it; dive into it. The Lord is our strength; the Lord is our support; the Lord is our sustainer; the Lord is our Savior.

Yes, salvation is *of* the Lord, *through* the Lord, *by* the Lord, and *from* the Lord. From beginning to end it's all grace.

Through the rest of this book we'll find out exactly how God's grace works in our lives, but let's be sure we have the foundation clear: we have been saved by grace, we now live by grace, and forever we will enjoy the riches of God's grace.

It's only understandable, then, that a glorious concept like this could be abused. Even the New Testament writers dealt with this abuse several times, with Paul giving an emphatic no to two theoretical questions about grace from the Romans. (See Romans 6, where Paul responds to the questions: "Should we sin more, so that there will more grace?" and, "Are we now free to sin, since we're not under the law but under grace?")

Jude also dealt with the abuse of grace, writing, "I say this because some ungodly people have wormed their way into your churches, saying that God's marvelous grace allows us to live immoral lives. The condemnation of such people was recorded long ago, for they have denied our only Master and Lord, Jesus Christ" (Jude 1:4, NLT).

So it's clear that grace can be abused, and the best way to avoid the abuse of grace is to get to know biblical grace—God's grace—intimately for ourselves. The more we know the authentic, the better equipped we will be to avoid the exaggerated and counterfeit.

Chapter 2

ARE ALL OUR SINS— PAST, PRESENT, AND FUTURE—ALREADY FORGIVEN IN JESUS?

I see that the Scriptures teach that in the new covenant, under grace, God forgives all my sins and remembers them no more. Does that mean He has already forgiven me for the sins I will commit for the rest of my life?

ONE OF THE foundations of the modern grace message is that the moment we are saved, God forgives all of our sins, meaning past sins, present sins, and future sins. In fact, some hyper-grace teachers claim that God doesn't even see the sins we commit as believers since He sees us as completely sanctified and holy in His Son.[1] To back up this position up, they commonly quote the words of the new covenant prophecy spoken in Jeremiah 31:31–34 and repeated in Hebrews 8:8–12, culminating with these words: "For I will be merciful toward their iniquities, and *I will remember their sins no more*" (ESV, emphasis added), a phrase that is quoted again in Hebrews 10:17—"I will remember their sins and their lawless deeds no more."

It is true that when Jesus died on the cross, He paid for every sin that you and I and the rest of the human race would ever commit, from Adam's first sin until the very last sin that will be committed on this planet. But that doesn't mean God forgives our sins before we commit them.

That is not taught anywhere in the Bible. When the Lord says He forgives us and remembers our sins no more, He's speaking of the sins we have committed at the time He forgives us.

The New Testament is totally clear on this. As it is written in 2 Peter 1, the believer who goes backward spiritually rather than forward "is nearsighted and blind, forgetting that they have been cleansed *from their past sins*" (2 Pet. 1:9, NIV, emphasis added; the English Standard Version reads, "...having forgotten that he was cleansed from his former sins").

What sins did God forgive when we asked Him to save and cleanse us? He forgave our past sins, our former sins, the sins we committed before we were born again. As Colossians 2 explains, when we put our faith in Jesus and became children of God, He canceled "the record of debt that stood against us with its legal demands. This he set aside, nailing it to the cross" (v. 14, ESV). The Complete Jewish Bible says "He wiped away the bill of charges against us," and the New International Version puts it this way: "Having canceled the charge of our legal indebtedness, which stood against us and condemned us; he has taken it away, nailing it to the cross."

Under the law we accumulated a massive amount of spiritual debt, with each new sin we committed adding to that debt. And it was a debt we could never repay, especially since the standards of God's law continually reminded us of our failures and shortcomings. (See chapter 6 for more on this.) But the moment God saved us, He forgave us that debt—some scholars refer to it as an IOU—and then He brought us into a new and better covenant, one in which His laws are written on our hearts, and He remembers our sins no more (Jer. 31:31–34).

So when we look to the Lord for salvation, He forgives every sin we have committed up to that point, and He even forgives us for who we are: lost, rebellious sinners. But He does not forgive us for our sins before we commit them. This is clearly stated in many passages, and it makes perfect spiritual sense as well.

Before we look at some additional scriptures, let me ask you a simple question. When you put your trust in Jesus as your Savior and Lord and you asked Him to forgive you for all your sins, what sins did you mean? Perhaps you said something like, "God, I confess to You that I am a sinner and have done many wrong things in my life, and I ask You to forgive me and wash me clean."

Is that how you prayed? I said something similar to the Lord, and He met me right where I was as a heroin-shooting, LSD-using, rebellious, hippie rock drummer. I was clean and forgiven and washed at that very moment. Totally! And all the guilt I had been feeling in previous weeks as the Holy Spirit was convicting me of my sins was totally gone as well. What amazing grace!

But it didn't dawn on me to say, "And Lord, while we're at it, could You please forgive me for all the sins I plan to commit tomorrow and for the rest of my life, along with the sins I don't plan to commit?"

I bet it didn't dawn on you to say that either. Why? It is because we understand that forgiveness is for what we have done, not for what we will do.

In the same way, if I sinned against my friend and let him down, I would go to him and say, "Please forgive me for being irresponsible and causing you pain. I was wrong, and I make no excuses." But I wouldn't say to him, "And since I'm confessing and you're forgiving, I ask you to forgive me in advance for every sin I will ever commit against you in the future as well." Of course not!

You might say, "But isn't it different with God, since He sees the future the way we see the past?" Not at all, even though He inhabits eternity (Isa. 57:15) and knows the beginning from the end (Isa. 46:8–10). When it comes to forgiveness, He forgives people only for what they have done, not what they will do. Consequently *there is not a single verse in the Bible where God forgives a person's sins before they commit those sins.* Not one.

To repeat: Jesus *paid for* all our sins when He hung on the cross, which means that for all of us living after the Cross, He paid for our sins before we were ever born. But He does not forgive our sins until we come to Him asking for mercy, and when He forgives us, He forgives what we have done.

To give a simple analogy, let's say I put one million dollars into a special account for a person's education, telling the student that whenever he incurred a debt for tuition, textbooks, or living expenses while in college, he could just send me a text with the amount and I'd transfer the funds into his account. The funds are there and the provision is made in advance, but the money isn't transferred until the debt is incurred.

In the same way, forgiveness covers whatever "debt" we have incurred, which is why Jesus taught us to pray, "Forgive us our debts, as we forgive our debtors" (Matt. 6:12). We are not encouraged to forgive debts not yet incurred.

(For the question of how we apply Jesus's words to our lives today, see chapter 10.)

If you look at every single prayer for forgiveness recorded in the Bible, you will see that people (and nations) ask for forgiveness only for what they have done, not what they will do. Then look at every single time God pronounces a person or nation forgiven in the Bible, and you will see that, without exception, it is for sins that person or nation has already committed, not for future sins.

Grace in Action

I know some teachers today say, "God doesn't forgive in installments," and it sounds very powerful. But that teaching has no basis in Scripture. In fact, the entire Bible is against it.

That being said, it *is* true that God doesn't *save* in installments, meaning that the moment He says, "I forgive you," you become a child of God and you pass from death to life, from the kingdom of Satan to the kingdom of God, from condemned to not guilty, from wicked to righteous, from lost to saved, from having a debt of sins bigger than Mount Everest to being totally and absolutely forgiven—all in a moment of time. That is grace in action. That is the power of the blood of Jesus. It is a free gift, and it is yours forever.

That also means that if you sin tomorrow and get upset with a coworker, you do not become unsaved and go back to death, back to the kingdom of Satan, back to being condemned, back to being wicked and lost. Instead, as a child of God who is still in the "forgiven" column—meaning God looks at you as His beloved child, a former guilty sinner whom He has pronounced forgiven—you now need to apply the blood of Jesus to your life and receive fresh cleansing. But you do *not* do this as a lost sinner being saved. Rather, you do it as a child of God who is in the "saved-righteous-holy-forgiven" column, freshly applying that source of forgiveness—the blood of Jesus—to your life again.

It is important to understand clearly that God does not forgive our sins before we commit them, since this false teaching opens the door to all kinds of deception and danger. You see, if I really believe that my future sins are already forgiven, in a time of weakness or temptation I might think to myself, "It's no big deal if I do that, since I'm already forgiven and therefore nothing could change my relationship with God, no matter what I do." I think you can see how dangerous that could be.

To explain this further, we know that God doesn't dredge up our past to condemn us, reminding us every day, "You were a terrible wretch before you were saved, and you did some really bad things. You should feel ashamed of yourself." That is not our Father! We *did* do terrible things before we were saved, and we *did* feel ashamed, but all that is forgiven and forgotten.

But what if I believed the same thing about my future sins? That would mean that when the Holy Spirit came to make me feel uncomfortable, warning me of danger, I would ignore the Spirit's loving work, thinking it was my own mind or, worse still, attributing it to the devil:

"God already forgave me for this sin, so the Holy Spirit wouldn't convict me." And so, rather than heeding the Spirit's rebuke—which is meant to be life-saving—I will plunge headlong into disaster.

It would be like a driver saying, "By faith I've already arrived at my destination, so I can ignore these warning signs on the road." In reality, we ignore them to our own peril. (For more on this, see chapter 4.)

THE PRICE FOR FORGIVENESS HAS BEEN PAID

That being said, modern grace teachers make a very good point when they remind us that God deals with us as His children, which means that we don't get saved one moment, become lost the next moment (the moment we commit a sin), and then get "resaved" the moment we ask for forgiveness. This kind of spiritual schizophrenia is not only totally unbiblical, but it is also totally maddening. Who can possibly live like this?

So it is crucial that we find a place of security in the Lord, remembering that we are saved by grace, not by works; by God's goodness, not by our goodness. It's also crucial to understand that when God forgives, He forgets—meaning He doesn't keep a record of wrongs against us—and that when we are forgiven, we are really forgiven. And it's crucial to understand that Jesus paid the price for every sin we will ever commit, and when we come to Him in sincerity, asking Him to wash us clean, He will do so without hesitation. The price has already been paid.

This means that if God isn't bringing up your past, you shouldn't bring it up either, and if He says you are forgiven, you really are forgiven. Receive it, no matter what you've done and no matter how far you've fallen. And shout it out for the world to hear: "I am God's child, and I am forgiven!"

You might grieve deeply over the sins you committed, and that is commendable. Could you imagine a husband who committed adultery not grieving deeply over his sin when he repents to

God and to his wife? You might feel sorrowful when you think back to some foolish thing you did in the recent past, one that brought terrible hardship on you and others, and you might kick yourself, thinking, "How in the world could I have been so stupid?" That is totally understandable.

But at the same time you should know that God really has forgiven you, that He really does love you, that He doesn't put you in the doghouse, that you don't need to get saved again, and that He doesn't want you to wallow in guilt. Just consider the parable of the Pharisee and the tax collector in Luke 18:9–14. The Pharisee, a respected religious practitioner, boasted to the Lord about his own righteous works. In contrast, the tax collector, recognizing his guilt, wouldn't even lift his head when he prayed. Instead, he beat his breast and said, "God, be merciful to me a sinner."

Those simple words, "God, be merciful to me a sinner," were the only words that tax collector needed to pray. Jesus says it was this man—the sinful tax collector, not the religious

Pharisee—who went home justified. Amazing! That is the grace of God, and to repeat, when He forgives, He forgets. As the Scriptures declare:

> Blessed is he whose transgression is forgiven, whose sin is covered. Blessed is the man against whom the LORD does not count iniquity, and in whose spirit there is no deceit.
> —PSALM 32:1–2

> I have blotted out, as a thick cloud, your transgressions, and your sins, as a cloud. Return to Me, for I have redeemed you.
> —ISAIAH 44:22

> For I will forgive their iniquity, and I will remember their sin no more.
> —JEREMIAH 31:34

> Who is a God like You, bearing iniquity and passing over transgression for the remnant of His inheritance? He does not remain angry forever, because He delights in benevolence. He will again have compassion upon us. He will tread

down our iniquities, and cast all of our
sins into the depths of the sea.

—MICAH 7:18–19

And here is something remarkable: all the
verses I just cited are from the Old Testament,
with the authors still looking forward to the fullness of forgiveness that comes to us through the
Cross. How much more, then, can we be confident that our own sins are forgiven in Jesus once
and for all!

So you can rest assured that, as far as your salvation is concerned, you have been forgiven of
your sins, and God remembers them no more.
How mind-boggling is that? And as for your
ongoing relationship with God, forgiveness is
applied whenever we need it and ask for it.

To illustrate this point, let me take you back to
December 1971 when God graciously saved me
from my sins. Although I first made a profession
of faith on November 12, 1971, this profession
was more of an (unexpected) acknowledgment
that I actually believed Jesus died for me. Prior
to that I would have dismissed the idea. But

when I professed my faith that Friday night in November, it was only a first step, since I wasn't willing to follow Jesus or turn away from my sinful lifestyle.

It was on December 17, 1971, that the break-through came, and it was a glorious break-through I can never forget. The Lord met me so wonderfully that night—it was also a Friday night—and I knew beyond a doubt that my slate was clear and my heart was clean. I was totally forgiven, even before I went home and threw out my needles and the drugs I used to shoot into my veins. All my guilt was gone, and in God's sight I was like a newborn child.

For me, the point of surrender was to say to the Lord, "I will never put a needle in my arm again," since that was the principal battle in my soul, the principal area where I had been unwilling to say yes to the Lord. But on that glo-rious night in December, my heart was so filled with the love and joy of the Lord that it was easy for me to make that commitment, and by His grace I was free from that night on.

A couple of days later, while hanging out with some friends, I got high, smoking hash (hashish), and not really thinking much about it. But a few hours later, riding home alone on the bus, I felt convicted in my heart that this too was displeasing before God. I asked Him to forgive me and told Him I would give up all drugs, not just those I shot intravenously.

But this is what I want you to grasp. I was still saved and forgiven while smoking hash that day. I didn't ask God to forgive me for getting high that day because I needed to get saved all over again. It was because I realized that my actions were displeasing in His sight, and more than anything I wanted to honor Jesus with the way I lived.

It took some weeks before I realized that profanity was sinful (to be perfectly honest with you, I was such a rebel and so full of ugliness that there were quite a few other things the Lord dealt with me about before He began to convict me of my foul speech), and thankfully I haven't used profanity in more than forty-four years. It's really the last thing on my mind. But, to use this as an example, if, God forbid, I uttered a profane word today, of course I would be instantly convicted by the Spirit, and of course I would instantly apologize to the Lord (and anyone who heard me utter the word), asking for immediate forgiveness. But I would not need to get saved all over again.

Why then would I ask for forgiveness? Once again, this would be the forgiveness of relationship, not the forgiveness of salvation. I received that once and for all the night Jesus saved me from my sins, and it is only by rejecting Him as Lord and turning my back on that forgiveness that I could forfeit His precious gift. (For more on the question of "losing" our salvation, see chapter 12.)

Because modern grace teachers often fail to distinguish between the forgiveness of salvation and the forgiveness of relationship (some even mock the distinction), they teach erroneously that even our future sins are pronounced forgiven the moment we are saved. Now that we have seen the error of that teaching in this chapter, we'll focus in the next chapter on receiving forgiveness for the sins we commit day to day and that affect our walk with the Father.

Chapter 3

IF A BELIEVER FAILS TO CONFESS EVEN ONE SIN BEFORE HE DIES, WILL HE GO TO HELL?

Sometimes I'm afraid that if I fall asleep at night without confessing all the sins I committed during the day and I died during the middle of the night, I will go to hell. That really scares me and takes away my peace.

I T IS COMMON to hear modern grace teachers say that as Christians we no longer need to confess our sins to God because we are already righteous in Him. After all, according to them, any future sins we may commit are already forgiven. So rather than confess our sins, they say we should simply rejoice in our perpetual righteousness in Christ.

This sounds nice, especially for those who suffer from a continually guilty conscience, always feeling inadequate, never believing they've done enough to please God, and feeling as though they are always falling short. The idea that God always sees them as perfect and holy because they are now in the "saved, righteous child of God" column is liberating. But as explained in chapter 2, there is a difference between the forgiveness of salvation and the forgiveness of relationship that comes through acknowledging and confessing our sins to God.

I've also seen many believers labor under the conception that if they die in their sleep without having confessed every last sin, they would go to hell. This too is an erroneous extreme, but the hyper-grace teachers go to another erroneous extreme in their zeal to correct this error.

As we saw in the last chapter, the moment we are born again, God puts us in the "saved, forgiven, righteous child of God" column. As far as our salvation is concerned, we are forgiven, once and for all. We are no longer considered enemies of God; we are considered friends of God (Isa. 41:8; John 15:9–17), and unless we willfully choose to renounce Jesus as Lord and leave the family of God, we are secure forever.

That means that as far as our salvation is concerned, we never have to worry about being forgiven of our sins again. Consequently, if we sin as a believer, we don't need to get "resaved" any more than we need to get "re-baptized." That's a big difference between believers under grace and believers under the Sinai covenant in the Old Testament (the covenant initiated in Moses's day). As Hebrews explains:

> For the law is a shadow of the good things to come, and not the very image of those things. It could never by the same sacrifices, which they offer continually year after year, perfect those who draw near. Otherwise, would they not have ceased to be offered, since the worshippers, once purified, would no longer be conscious of sins? But in those sacrifices there is an annual reminder of sins. For it is not possible for the blood of bulls and goats to take away sins
>
> —Hebrews 10:1–4

The children of Israel needed an annual Day of Atonement to receive forgiveness on a national level, which means they never experienced the "once and for all" forgiveness we experience in Jesus. They certainly did understand the concept of mercy and forgiveness, and this is celebrated in the Old Testament in many passages on both an individual and national level. (See, for example, Daniel 9:1–19.) But, to repeat, the idea of being made right with God for life through a one-time act of faith and repentance was unknown to them.

Not only so, but Jewish tradition emphasizes that the forgiveness Israel received every year on the Day of Atonement was directly tied to the sincerity of the nation's repentance. If they didn't truly repent, their sins would not be forgiven, and every year the cycle would be repeated. (See the Babylonian Talmud, Yoma 39a-b.[1]) Things are wonderfully different for us in Jesus! "For if the blood of bulls and goats, and the ashes of a heifer, sprinkling the unclean, sanctifies so that the flesh is purified, how much more shall the blood of Christ, who through the eternal Spirit offered Himself without blemish to God, cleanse your conscience from dead works to serve the living God?" (Heb. 9:13–14).

Think for a moment about water baptism. It symbolizes the washing away of our sins (Acts 22:16), is tied in to the forgiveness of our sins (Acts 2:38), and depicts our dying to sin and rising to new life in Jesus (Rom. 6:3–5). What happens if we sin once we are baptized? Do we need to get baptized again? If so, that would mean we would need to get baptized on a regular basis—a daily if not an hourly basis—since all of us fall short of God's perfect holiness one way or another every day of our lives. When is the last time you lived twenty-four straight hours loving God perfectly with all your heart, soul, and strength; loving all your neighbors as yourself and never sinning in thought, word, or deed, including both sins of commission (what you did do) and sins of omission (what you failed to do)?

It's the same with our salvation. We don't need to get resaved every time we sin. He has saved us once and for all, and we now belong to Him as dearly loved children.

So as a believer in Jesus, my mind-set and posture before God is that I am His child, that I am loved by Him, and that all my past sins have been forgiven. As Paul described, "Once you were alienated from God and were enemies in your minds because of your evil behavior" (Col. 1:21, NIV). Yes, "you were dead in your trespasses and sins, in which you formerly walked according to the age of this world and according to the prince of the power of the air, the spirit who now works in the sons of disobedience, among them we all also once lived in the lusts of our flesh, doing the desires of the flesh and of the mind, and we were by nature children of wrath, even as the rest" (Eph. 2:1–3).

Thankfully, that is not the end of the story. "But God, being rich in mercy, because of His great love with which He loved us, even when we were dead in sins, made us alive together with Christ (by grace you have been saved), and He raised us up and seated us together in the heavenly places in Christ Jesus, so that in the coming ages He might show the surpassing riches of His grace in kindness toward us in Christ Jesus" (vv. 4–7).

If you want to understand grace, just read these glorious verses over and over. They shout out the incredible message from the rooftops. As Paul continues, "For by grace you have been saved through faith, and this is not of yourselves. It is the gift of God, not of works, so that no one should boast" (Eph. 2:8–9). What an amazing gift!

So, as far as your salvation is concerned, you are forgiven once and for all. That mountain of debt you carried so long has been wiped out, and the Judge has pronounced the verdict, "Not guilty!" You can rest assured of this. Even when you struggle with sin, you come to God as His beloved child rather than as a hostile outsider. As Paul wrote in Romans 8, "Who shall bring a charge against God's elect? It is God who justifies. Who is he who condemns? It is Christ who died, yes, who is risen, who is also at the right hand of God, who also intercedes for us" (vv. 33–34). The case against you has been dismissed, and Jesus is pleading your cause.

And this is where the question of *ongoing confession and forgiveness* becomes relevant: it is part of our relationship with God, part of being in His family. And so, in the same way a daughter comes to her mother and asks for her forgiveness when she has done something wrong, we come to God asking for His forgiveness when we have done something wrong. And just as that daughter does not say to her mother, "Please make me your daughter again," we don't say, "Please save me again." This is the forgiveness that takes place within the family, the forgiveness of relationship.

Many Christians have the mistaken notion that if they died while committing a sin—for instance, getting angry with a driver who cut them off on the road, then getting killed in the ensuing car accident—they would go to hell. They think that if they didn't have time to repent of that sin, they would be damned.

But that is not taught anywhere in the Scriptures, and it brings bondage and fear more than it brings freedom. To be sure, I would hate to think of leaving this world while in a state of sin, but our salvation does not hinge on dying at the right moment or being sure that we confessed every last sin before we fell asleep at night.

To be clear, I'm not talking about a believer turning his or her back on Jesus and choosing a life of sin and rebellion, rejecting Him as Lord and refusing to repent. If we reject Him, He will reject us.

I'm talking about a child of God who wants to please the Father. He understands our struggles and our weaknesses (Ps. 103:13–14), and He simply wants us to come to Him in humility when we fall short, confessing our sins (He loves honesty!), confessing His goodness (we are reminding ourselves more than we are reminding Him), and receiving a fresh cleansing from our sins.

As it is written in 1 John 1:8–10, "If we say that we have no sin, we deceive ourselves, and the truth is not in us. If we confess our sins, He is faithful and just to forgive us our sins and cleanse us from all unrighteousness. If we say that we have not sinned, we make Him a liar and His word is not in us."

JOHN AND THE GNOSTICS

Who is John addressing here? There are some teachers today who claim he was addressing a group of heretics called the Gnostics, a pseudo-Christian group who claimed they did not sin (among other false beliefs). But this group did not come into existence until some years after John's letter was written, so this passage can't refer to them. And even if such a group did exist back then—the seeds of their beliefs were clearly beginning to circulate in John's day—it is clear John is not addressing them because he refers to "we" and "us" rather than "they" and "them."

Take a few minutes and read through 1 John (it's a very short letter), and note every time John speaks of himself, the other leaders, or believers in Jesus in general. He always speaks of "we" and "us" and "our," and he writes to "you." Then note how he addresses the nonbelievers. He speaks of "them," not "us." *They* are the outsiders who have left the flock; *you* are the insiders who are part of God's flock. *We* are the family of God together; *they* are not. So it is clear that John is not writing to outsiders but to insiders when he says, "If we confess our sins, He is faithful and just to forgive us our sins and cleanse us from all unrighteousness" (1 John 1:9).

Is it possible, though, that John was first giving an invitation to salvation in this opening chapter, knowing that there would be nonbelievers who would hear this letter being read in the churches, and was speaking to them gently, using such language as "we" and "our" and "us"? Actually, that's not possible, not only because it violates the way these words are used throughout the letter but also because the Greek itself forbids it.

You see, the ancient Greek language has a very precise verbal system, more precise than the English language and much more precise than the Hebrew language, which has a more fluid verbal system. That means a Greek author could distinguish very clearly between a past action that was completed ("It rained yesterday"), a past action that was still continuing ("It has been raining since yesterday"), a present continuous action ("The sun rises every morning"), and future actions ("The sun will rise tomorrow").

The Greek can be much more precise; I'm just giving simple examples here.

In the case of 1 John 1:9 the Greek speaks of a *present continuous action*: if, on a regular basis, we confess our sins, then, on a regular basis, God will forgive us our sins and cleanse us from all unrighteousness.

This does *not* refer to a one-time invitation to salvation, as in, "If you're hearing these words and you don't know the Lord, confess your sins to Him and ask Him to forgive you, and He will do so." Instead, it refers to our ongoing relationship with Him, as in, "When you sin and dishonor the Lord, confess your sin to Him and He will wash you clean."

You might ask, "But aren't I clean already? Didn't the blood of Jesus wash me clean when I got saved? I thought that was the whole meaning of the old hymn 'Are You Washed in the Blood?'"

Yes, you *have been cleansed* in the once-for-all sense of being saved from your sins, but on a relational basis, you *still need to be cleansed*. Put another way, when it comes to your salvation, you are cleansed from head to toe the moment you are born again. When it comes to your relationship with God, you need to get your feet washed on a regular basis, since, as we live in this world, our feet get dirty. In Paul's words (speaking to believers), "Let us cleanse ourselves from all filthiness of the flesh and spirit" (2 Cor. 7:1). This means that as children of God, we can still get defiled in this world, but there is mercy and grace to cleanse us from that defilement.

As followers of Jesus, then, we are called to keep ourselves unstained by the world. (See Jacob [James] 1:27.) But when we do get stained, we don't need to get saved again; we simply need to get our feet washed.

Jesus explained this concept in John 13 when He literally washed the disciples' feet. To give the context, Jesus knew He was about to be betrayed and that He was about to return to God. Before He left this world, He wanted to show His disciples the full extent of His love. (See John 13:1–3.) So what did He do? He "rose from supper, laid aside His garments, and took a towel and wrapped Himself. After that, He poured water into a basin and began to wash the disciples' feet and to wipe them with the towel with which He was wrapped" (John 13:4–5).

This was too much for Simon Peter: "Lord," he exclaimed, "there's no way You're going to wash my feet!" But Jesus insisted: "Unless I wash you, you have no part with Me." This left impetuous Peter with only one response: "Then, Lord, not just my feet but my hands and my head as well!" (See John 13:6–9.) Amen, Peter! You're my kind of guy—all or nothing at all, both feet in or both feet out. Peter was saying, "If getting my feet washed is essential to staying in right relationship with You, then wash my whole body. Give me the whole package, Lord!"

Jesus answered him, "'He who is bathed needs only to wash his feet, but is completely clean. You are clean, but not all of you.' For He knew who would betray Him. Therefore He said, 'Not all of you are clean'" (John 13:10–11).

What did Jesus mean? Well, you need to remember the culture of the day. The houses back then didn't have running water or plumbing, and that meant homes had no private showers or baths. When you wanted to bathe, you would either go to the river or to a public bath house. There you would wash and get completely clean. But then you had to walk back home, and that meant trekking down grimy, dusty roads. No matter what you did, your feet would get dirty. So when you arrived at someone's house, it was a customary act of kindness for them to have a basin of water ready and a servant waiting to wash your feet. But that didn't mean you needed to take another bath. You only needed to get your feet washed.

How did Jesus apply this spiritually? Well, all of His disciples (except Judas, who was about to betray Him) were in good standing with Him. He had received them as His own, forgiving their sins, and in His words, they were already "clean." (See also John 15:3, "You are already clean through the word which I have spoken to you.") Their head, hands, and whole body were bathed. They needed only to have their feet washed.

"That's nice," you say, "but I still don't get it. What does this have to do with 1 John 1:7?"

Simply this: When we get saved, we get bathed from head to toe. God cleans us up big-time, scrubbing away the accumulated filth. And there is a lot of filth to wash away! For some of us it amounted to decades of sin and pollution—in other words, decades without a bath. Can you imagine, spiritually speaking, how miserably we stunk when we first asked God for mercy?

I think immediately of the roadside beggars I have often seen on my annual ministry trips to India. It is difficult to describe the utter squalor in which these people live. Dressed in torn clothes (or sometimes just soiled rags) that look as if they have been soaked in motor oil, they are covered with dirt (and sometimes sores), and their long hair is stiff and totally matted. (God only knows what kind of little creatures live in that hair.) I once asked one of my Indian friends, "Why don't they shave their heads instead? Wouldn't they be more comfortable?" He explained, "No, they leave their hair like that to get more money begging." Really, it's hard to describe just how repulsive and tragic a sight it is.

Yet that's how we looked when we got saved! We were utterly repulsive, coated with grime, a mass of "wounds and welts and open sores, not cleansed or bandaged or soothed with olive oil" (Isa. 1:6, NIV). And in one moment of time, when we put our faith in the Lord Jesus and asked Him to save us from our sins, He healed our sick spirits and made us white as snow. He made us pure and holy. He made us clean!

This is what the Word says: "You were washed, you were sanctified, and you were justified in the name of the Lord Jesus by the Spirit of our God" (1 Cor. 6:11). Yes, Jesus cleansed us "with the washing of water by the word" (Eph. 5:26) and "saved us, through the washing of rebirth and the renewal of the Holy Spirit" (Titus 3:5). Now, we can "draw near with a true heart in full assurance of faith, having our hearts sprinkled to cleanse them from an evil conscience, and our bodies washed with pure water" (Heb. 10:22).

There's only one problem: We still live in this world. We still have to walk along dusty, dirty roads, and sometimes our feet get dirty, even though we have been washed and bathed. There is simply no way to avoid all the dirt all the time. It's like going into a room filled with cigarette smokers. Even though you don't smoke yourself, you come out smelling like smoke—and some of the fumes get into your lungs too. That's a picture of the polluting power of sin.

Sometimes we are enveloped by profanity on a job site, even though we ourselves never utter such words. Still, just hearing filth can make you feel unclean. Other times we find ourselves coming into contact with people whose dress and behavior are lewd and sensual, and we feel dragged down by their sinful ways, even though we have kept ourselves morally upright. We feel dirty. But that doesn't mean we need another bath! We just need to get our feet washed. We just need to pray, "Father, cleanse me from this junk, in Jesus's name!" Purification in the Bible can be for uncleanness as well as for sin.

Yet there are times when we do sin, and that means getting our feet get dirty—even though we are walking in the light and our lives are no longer dominated by disobedience and self-will. The fact is, every day all of us fall short to one extent or another. Perhaps we have a fleeting thought of envy or competition, or maybe we speak a judgmental word about a fellow believer or fail to focus on the Lord during prayer. Perhaps the problem one day is our lack of compassion for a church member in need, or maybe we cast a fleeting, lustful glance at someone or momentarily become swelled with pride because the Lord saw fit to use us.

One way or another, even as consecrated, dedicated, separated children of God, we still have some momentary blemishes and spots. But that doesn't mean we need to get saved again every time we fall short. Instead, we immediately turn to the Lord for cleansing, wiping the grime from our feet as soon as we recognize it, and receiving mercy and grace from His hand.

Chapter 4

DOES THE HOLY SPIRIT CONVICT BELIEVERS OF SIN?

I know John 16:8 says the Holy Spirit convicts the world of sin, but does the Spirit convict believers of sin? When I think of being "convicted," I think of being pronounced guilty, and if I'm God's child, why would He pronounce me guilty?

ONE OF THE most common teachings within hyper-grace circles is that the Holy Spirit does not convict believers of sin, since God has already forgiven and forgotten all our sins and sees us as perfect in Jesus. This may come as a relief to those who constantly feel they are never doing enough for God and are always missing the mark. But dismissing the Holy Spirit's correction is not the way to silence the lies of Satan, the accuser. God loves us too much to sit back and allow sin to damage and destroy us.

Conviction is good, not bad, something sent from heaven, not manufactured in hell. Yet many people fail to realize that because they confuse conviction with condemnation, though the two are very different.

One of the most glorious truths of the New Testament is that there is "no condemnation for those who are in Christ Jesus" (Rom. 8:1). That means the Holy Spirit will *never* say to us as children of God, "You are a guilty sinner. Off to hell with you!" He will never condemn us, nor will

He make us feel like lost, hopeless sinners. That is not what He does, and that is not who we are.

But He will absolutely make us feel uncomfortable when we sin (in particular, if we persist in willful, unrepentant sin), and He will certainly correct us when we sin. This is what I mean when I say the Holy Spirit convicts us of our sins as believers. He makes us feel uneasy; He brings a word of loving rebuke; He puts us under holy pressure—all because He loves us so much! It's like the rough gravel on the side of the highway that tells you you're getting off the road. It gets your attention—both with the sound and with the feel—waking you up to the potential danger of an imminent crash. That gravel can save your life.

Let's take a look at John 16:8, where Jesus said that when the Holy Spirit comes, He "will convict the world concerning sin and righteousness and judgment" (NAS). Other Bible translations that use the word *convict* include the Modern English Version, New King James Version, English Standard Version, and New

Living Translation. But while this is a perfectly acceptable way to translate the word, to some readers it sounds like a courtroom verdict where a person is "convicted" of a crime. In contrast, the King James Version says He will "reprove the world of sin," while the New International Version states that He will "prove the world to be in the wrong about sin." (See also the New English Translation and New Revised Standard Version, which have very similar wording; the Complete Jewish Bible says He will "show that the world is wrong about sin.")

With this in mind, we can ask the question, "Does the Holy Spirit prove us to be in the wrong concerning sin? Does He show us that our actions are wrong? Does He correct us and make us uncomfortable?" Of course He does! If He failed to do this, God would not be a good Father. Hebrews 12 tells us:

> In your struggle against sin you have not yet resisted to the point of shedding your blood. And have you forgotten the exhortation that addresses you as sons?

"My son, do not regard lightly the discipline of the Lord, nor be weary when reproved by him. For the Lord disciplines the one he loves, and chastises every son whom he receives." It is for discipline that you have to endure. God is treating you as sons. For what son is there whom his father does not discipline? If you are left without discipline, in which all have participated, then you are illegitimate children and not sons. Besides this, we have had earthly fathers who disciplined us and we respected them. Shall we not much more be subject to the Father of spirits and live? For they disciplined us for a short time as it seemed best to them, but he disciplines us for our good, that we may share his holiness. For the moment all discipline seems painful rather than pleasant, but later it yields the peaceful fruit of righteousness to those who have been trained by it.

—HEBREWS 12:4–11, ESV

The word translated "reprove" in verse 5 of this

The word translated "reprove" in verse 5 of this quote is the same exact Greek word translated "convict" in John 16:8. *The Scriptures are stating explicitly that the Holy Spirit does this very work in the lives of God's children.* This is the proof that we belong to Him.

God Disciplines Those He Loves

When I see a stranger's children misbehaving in a mall, as much as I might like to, it's not my place to correct them. But it is my place to do so with my own kids, especially when they're in my home. To fail to do so would be to fail my children, since failing to address sinful behavior only leads to more sinful behavior, and more sinful behavior can lead to disaster.

That's why Jesus, speaking by the Spirit, said in Revelation 3:19, "Those whom I love, I reprove and discipline, so be zealous and repent" (ESV). And note once again the word *reprove*: it's the exact same word in the Greek as the word sometimes translated *convict* in John 16:8 and

Hebrews 12:5. This reproof and correction is a clear sign of God's love.

Isn't it strange, then, that some teachers claim that God will *not* convict His people of sin *because* He loves us? It's the exact opposite! It is *because* He loves us that He *does* convict us of our sins. To fail to do so would be to fail in His parenting responsibilities.

One modern grace teacher stated that the Spirit would never make us uncomfortable for our sins because the Spirit is called the "Comforter" in the New Testament, but this argument is both unscriptural and illogical. First, almost no modern versions follow the King James Version in translating the Greek word *parakletos* with "Comforter." (See John 14:26.) Almost all of them use the word *Helper* (NKJV, NAS, ESV), Advocate (NIV, NET, NLT, NRSV), or Counselor (CJB, MEV). The Greek term carries the basic meaning of "one called alongside to help." So it is inaccurate to translate it "Comforter."

Second, even if one of the ministries of the Spirit is to comfort, which I certainly affirm, that doesn't mean that's the only thing He does. That would make no sense at all. There are times we need comfort, and there are times we need correction. There are times we need encouragement, and there are times we need rebuke. The Holy Spirit is here to help us through comfort or correction or encouragement or rebuke. Thank God for the ministry of the Spirit!

Paul explains that, when the Spirit is speaking to the church through prophecy "and an unbeliever or outsider enters, he is convicted by all, he is called to account by all, the secrets of his heart are disclosed, and so, falling on his face, he will worship God and declare that God is really among you" (1 Cor. 14:24–25, ESV). Note that the Greek word translated "convicted" in 1 Corinthians 14:24 is the same word, *elenchō*, we've been tracing through the New Testament that is also translated "reprove."

In this case the Spirit is convicting a nonbeliever of his sins, leading to his repentance and salvation. At other times the Spirit is convicting (or reproving) us as believers for our sins, leading to our repentance and restoration or saving us from death or disaster. To say it again, thank God for the ministry of the Spirit!

Many years ago I allowed some compromise into my life in one particular area (have you ever done that?), and I can tell you firsthand that the Holy Spirit made me miserable. I am eternally grateful that He did! The more I would pray and meet with God, the more uncomfortable I would become, since I was holding on to something displeasing in the Father's sight and it was contrary to who I was in Jesus. As for the peace that passes understanding promised us in the Word (Phil. 4:6–8), that was fleeting as well, since I harbored disobedience in my heart.

But the Holy Spirit never condemned me as if I was a lost sinner going to hell. He lovingly reproved me because, as a child of God, I was not called to compromise but to wholehearted devotion. And when I turned away from that compromise, it was as if the heavens were opened over me in an outpouring of grace. The Spirit's conviction was intense—I was on my face weeping in repentance, but that repentance was life-giving and precious. It was as if all the uncleanness was leaving me—the spiritual equivalent of a healthy dietary "purge"—and as a result my fellowship with Jesus was sweeter than it had been since I let that compromise enter my life.

This is similar to what happened with the Corinthians after Paul wrote to them about sin and compromise in their midst. He wrote with tears because of his love for them. He knew his words would hurt them, but he also knew his strong words would produce radical, lasting fruit. As he explained:

> For even if I made you grieve with my letter, I do not regret it—though I did regret it, for I see that that letter grieved you, though only for a while. As it is, I rejoice, not because you were grieved, but because you were grieved into repenting. For you felt a godly grief, so that you suffered no loss through us. For godly grief produces a repentance that leads to salvation without regret, whereas worldly grief produces death. For see what

earnestness this godly grief has pro-
duced in you, but also what eagerness to
clear yourselves, what indignation, what
fear, what longing, what zeal, what punishment! At every point you have proved
yourselves innocent in the matter.
—2 CORINTHIANS 7:8–11, ESV

The Holy Spirit brings us to a point of "godly
grief," and that godly grief helps us to turn away
from our sins and embrace God's beautiful holiness. And as we repent and ask for forgiveness,
the Spirit does His supernatural work in our
hearts, assuring us of the Father's love, com-
forting us with His kindness, and empowering
us to turn away from that which is ugly and
destructive. How wonderful the Spirit's work is!

Sometimes the issue is much more minor, and
we feel a gentle nudge from the Spirit showing
us (or reminding us) that we're heading in the
wrong direction. Sometimes the Spirit will speak
to us plainly through an internal witness, in a
dream or vision, or through a prophetic word.
But always the goal is the same: to keep us from

hurting ourselves, hurting others, and hurting the Lord. Conviction is a ministry of great love.

Condemnation says, "You have sinned. Get away from me!" Conviction says, "You have sinned. Come near me." The difference between the two is vast, as vast as the difference between death and life.

The Lord never pushes us away but always calls us near. That's how you can distinguish the convicting voice of the Spirit from the condemning voice of the enemy or even the condemning voice of your own mind (or of religious tradition). Condemnation pushes us away from the Lord. Conviction calls us near to Him.

Satan condemns, but the Spirit convicts; that is why I am so grateful to the Lord for this precious ministry of the Spirit. It is a lifesaver in every sense of the word, and rather than resisting it or denying it, we should embrace it. Conviction is the love of our Father in action on our behalf.

Chapter 5

DOES GOD SEE US AS RIGHTEOUS?

To me, the Bible is very practical, so I don't always understand what some theological terms mean, such as "positional righteousness." Does God see me as righteous or not?

WHERE ARE YOU right now as you read these words? Are you sitting in your favorite chair at home? Are you standing on a bus? Are you flying on a plane? Wherever you are physically, you are still here on earth—either on the ground or in the air—rather than in heaven. You are in a physical body, not a resurrected, spiritual body, and you are living in this world, not the world to come.

There is nothing controversial in my saying you're a human being living in this world. You need to sleep every day. You need to eat. You need money to pay bills. Whether you're married with children or single, you're part of the cycle of life in our world. You might attend a funeral one day, since everyone in this world dies, and you might attend a baby shower the next day, since babies are conceived every day, because this is the nature of life here on planet Earth.

Yet Paul wrote to the Ephesians, "But God, being rich in mercy, because of His great love with which He loved us, even when we were dead in sins, made us alive together with Christ (by grace you have been saved), and He raised us up and seated us together in the heavenly places in Christ Jesus" (Eph. 2:4–6). We just established that we're all living here on planet Earth. So what does it mean to be "raised up" and "seated together in the heavenly places in Christ"?

This passage reflects our *positional* standing in Jesus. Right now, in Him, we are seated in the heavenly places. This is a spiritual reality, not a fantasy. These verses speak of an actual spiritual state, not an imaginary condition. As Paul explained in Colossians 3, "If you then were raised with Christ, desire those things which are above, where Christ sits at the right hand of God. Set your affection on things above, not on things on earth. For you are dead, and your life is hidden with Christ in God. When Christ who is our life shall appear, then you also shall appear with Him in glory" (Col. 3:1–4).

Notice carefully what the Apostle Paul wrote to these believers: you were raised with the Messiah; you are dead; your life is now hidden with the Messiah in God. At the same time, we are still here on this earth, we are still physically alive, and we still have to deal with earthly things. That's why Paul writes in the very next verse, "Therefore put to death the parts of your earthly nature: sexual immorality, uncleanness, inordinate affection, evil desire, and covetousness, which is idolatry" (Col. 3:5). And that's why he continues exhorting the Colossians in practical terms: "You also once walked in these, when you lived in them. But now you must also put away all these: anger, wrath, malice, blasphemy, and filthy language out of your mouth. Do not lie one to another, since you have put off the old nature with its deeds, and have embraced the new nature, which is renewed in knowledge after the image of Him who created it" (vv. 7–10).

Do you understand Paul's point? In Jesus we have been given a new nature, which Paul describes in Ephesians 4:24 as "created according to God in righteousness and true holiness." But we still live in these bodies, in this fallen world, with minds that must be renewed. And so we must "put off" the old nature and "put on" the new nature. In other words, we must live out these spiritual realities here in this world.

Already but Not Yet

This is a constant theme of the New Testament, which speaks of "already but not yet" spiritual realities. As my friend and colleague Dr. Bob Gladstone explains:

> Failure to grasp the biblical tension of "already/not yet" is a failure to grasp biblical grace, and Jesus Himself. The kingdom is now; the kingdom is not yet. I am saved; I am being saved. The hour has come; the hour is yet future. I am sanctified; I am being sanctified. I am a new creation; I await resurrection. I am now a child of God; I am exhorted— sometimes warned—to endure to the end. So grace is both the virtue that saved me as a free gift and that governs me throughout the process of ongoing sanctification. But it never erases my

free will or the call to be a faithful steward.[1]

So we are already redeemed (Eph. 1:7) and we already have the Spirit, but at present the Spirit "is a deposit guaranteeing our inheritance *until* the redemption of those who are God's possession" (v. 14, NIV, emphasis added). We are already seated in heavenly places with Jesus (Eph. 2:6), but at present we are living in earthly bodies, because of which we groan (2 Cor. 5:2), "so that what is mortal might be swallowed up by life" (v. 4). We are already adopted as sons (Rom. 8:15), but for now, we "groan inwardly as we wait eagerly for adoption as sons, the redemption of our bodies" (v. 23, ESV).

We have already died to sin and cannot live in it any longer (Rom. 6:1–7), yet we must consider ourselves dead to sin and not let it rule in our lives (Rom. 6:11–19). We have already put off the old self and put on the new self (Eph. 4:22–24), yet we are instructed to "put to death" and "put off" that which pertains to our earthly nature and "put on" that which pertains to our new self (Col. 3:5–14, ESV). This is what is meant by "already and not yet."

And this is what I mean when I say "we *have been* sanctified, we *are being* sanctified, and *we will be* totally sanctified." (See chapter 8 for more on this.) As one theologian explained, our sanctification is *positional* (past), *progressive* (present), and *perfect* (future):

> Sanctification or Holiness of life has a threefold aspect: 1) Positional, which is past, through the work of Christ in our redemption, and confers upon the Christian a perfect position, as a child of God (Heb. 10:10); 2) Progressive, which is the present work of the Holy Spirit in the life of the believer, bringing one's character development into conformity with his position in Christ, and this is experiential throughout one's lifetime (2 Tim. 3:16–17; Col. 1:28; 2 Peter 3:18); 3) Perfection, which is future and will be completed when the Christian arrives in heaven, and then his character behaviors will be as perfect as his position

is in Christ (1 Thess. 3:12–13; Phil. 1:6;
1 John 3:2–3).[2]

Hyper-grace teachers reject the concept of
"positional righteousness" or "positional holiness,"
claiming that if our righteousness or holiness is
positional, it is not real. But this is a false and
unbiblical dichotomy. Spiritual realities are *real*,
but they are not yet fully *realized* while we live
in this body. We have one foot in this world and
one foot in the world to come. We have died to
sin, yet we still fight a battle with sin. (Anyone
telling you that he or she no longer has to deal
with sin—ever, in any form—is either lying to
you or self-deceived.) That's why Peter wrote in
1 Peter 2:11, "Dearly beloved, I implore you as
aliens and refugees, abstain from fleshly lusts,
which wage war against the soul." (He would not
have written this, nor would the New Testament
authors have written many other related verses,
if we were not in a battle.)

We have already been resurrected and raised
up spiritually with Jesus, yet we eagerly await
His appearing and our bodily resurrection. Our

lives are now "hidden with Christ in God" (Col. 3:3), yet we are living our lives openly in this world, seen by all. Both are simultaneously true, and the key is for these spiritual truths to so permeate our hearts and minds that we live them out here on earth.

Let's flesh this out by looking at Paul's teaching in Romans 6. Paul anticipated that his readers might misunderstand the message of grace, which is why he wrote:

> What shall we say then? Shall we continue in sin that grace may increase? God forbid! How shall we who died to sin live any longer in it? Do you not know that we who were baptized into Jesus Christ were baptized into His death? Therefore we were buried with Him by baptism into death, that just as Christ was raised up from the dead by the glory of the Father, even so we also should walk in newness of life.
>
> —ROMANS 6:1–4

I remember well the night I was baptized in water. It was February 4, 1972. After I came up out of the baptismal tank, one of the young ladies in the church smiled at me and said, "That water was really filthy after you were baptized."

For a moment I was shocked. Filthy? Really? Why?

Then I realized she was making a spiritual point: my sins, which were many and were utterly filthy, were now washed away, washed down the drain so to speak. As Ananias said to Saul/Paul, "Rise, be baptized and wash away your sins, and call on the name of the Lord" (Acts 22:16).

Baptism, then, symbolizes the washing away of our sins. As we go down into the water and come back up out of the water, it symbolizes our dying to sin, with Jesus, and our rising in new life, with Jesus. All this is a spiritual reality, and it speaks of our positional standing: we are dead to sin and raised up into new life. Now we must walk this reality out, since we are still living in physical bodies in this fallen world, a world in which Satan is still tempting and deceiving.

Paul continues, "Now if we died with Christ, we believe that we shall also live with Him, knowing that Christ, being raised from the dead, will never die again; death has no further dominion over Him. For the death He died, He died to sin once for all, but the life He lives, He lives to God" (Rom. 6:8–10). What does this mean on a practical level?

> Likewise, you also consider yourselves to be dead to sin, but alive to God through Jesus Christ our Lord. Therefore do not let sin reign in your mortal body, that you should obey it in its lusts. Do not yield your members to sin as instruments of unrighteousness, but yield yourselves to God, as those who are alive from the dead, and your bodies to God as instruments of righteousness. For sin shall not have dominion over you, for you are not under the law, but under grace.
> —ROMANS 6:11–14

We'll devote an entire chapter to verse 14, discussing what it means to be under grace, not the law (see chapter 6), but we'll focus here on verses 11–14. Here Paul explains that since we are (positionally) dead to sin, we need to consider that to be a reality, since it sure doesn't feel like we are dead to sin. After all, the drunkard in the coffin is not tempted in any way with alcohol, nor is the physical body of a dead adulterer tempted with lust. In that sense they have died to sin.

And that's exactly what Paul says has happened to us spiritually. We have already died to sin, just as surely as Jesus died on the cross, but we now have to take hold of that spiritual reality and live it out in the flesh. So Paul tells us to "consider ourselves" to be dead to sin and alive to God through Jesus, to "not let sin reign" in our mortal bodies, to "not yield" the parts of our body to sinful desires.

VICTORY IS REAL

The battle is real, and the victory is real. This is another example of "already but not yet" in the Bible. We have already been given complete and total victory over sin, but we have not yet experienced the totality of that victory in this world. If we had, there would never be temptation, sinful desires, or spiritual battles. In the same way, Satan was defeated at the Cross, but we are still in a battle with him in this age. The key for us is to take hold of our spiritual standing— seated with Jesus in heavenly places, equipped with the authority of Jesus's name—and from that place of victory to wage spiritual war.

I would encourage you to take a moment and read the rest of Romans 6, where Paul teaches us how to live these things out, as well as Ephesians 4–6 and Colossians 3. These chapters combine the spiritual with the practical, the realities of the age to come with the realities of this present age, presenting a balanced picture of what it means to be a child of God and how the Lord requires us to live. I would also encourage you to read all of Paul's letters carefully, looking for the phrase "in Christ" or "in Him," where Paul describes exactly who we are and where we stand in Jesus.

A few verses from Ephesians 1 indicate how incredibly rich these truths are:

> Blessed be the God and Father of our Lord Jesus Christ, who has blessed us with every spiritual blessing in the heavenly places *in Christ*, just as He chose us *in Him* before the foundation of the world, to be holy and blameless before Him in love; He predestined us to adoption as sons to Himself through Jesus Christ according to the good pleasure of His will, to the praise of the glory of His grace which He graciously bestowed on us *in the Beloved. In Him* we have redemption through His blood and the forgiveness of sins according to the riches of His grace.
>
> —EPHESIANS 1:3–7,
> EMPHASIS ADDED

Every good thing we have, we have in Jesus, and that is as true today as it ever will be. Yes, it's all about His blood and His grace, and that will be our boast throughout our lives in this world and in the world to come. But that is only one very real part of the story.

The other very real part of the story is that we are still living on planet Earth, which is why so much of the New Testament addresses how we are to live in this world. In keeping with that, Paul urges the Ephesians to take off their old nature, "which is corrupt according to the deceitful lusts," and to put on our new nature, "which was created according to God in righteousness and true holiness" (Eph. 4:22, 24).

What exactly does this mean? It means that we stop lying and instead speak the truth; that we control our tempers; that we give no place to the devil; that the thief stops stealing and instead works constructively; that we speak only edifying, life-giving words; that we not grieve the Holy Spirit. In short, "Let all bitterness, wrath, anger, outbursts, and blasphemies, with all malice, be taken away from you. And be kind one to another, tenderhearted, forgiving one another, just as God in Christ also forgave you" (vv. 31–32).

This, in fact, is just the beginning of Paul's practical exhortation, which continues in the fifth chapter, where we are exhorted to be imitators of the Lord, to be holy in our conduct, to walk and live as children of light, to submit one to another—for husbands to give themselves to their wives as Christ did for the church, for wives to submit to their husbands as to the Lord—and, continuing into chapter 6, for parents to lead their children rightly and for children to honor their parents. This is what it looks like when those seated in heavenly places in Jesus are still living here on this earth.

How then does God see us? Does He see us as righteous and holy, since, as we have stated a number of times already, the moment we are born again God declares us righteous and holy? Does He see us as perfect because we are now in Jesus, His perfect Son?

The answer to this is the answer to this whole chapter. It is yes and no, already and not yet. The Lord sees us as "righteous" in terms of being "not guilty." He does not always see our conduct as righteous. He sees us as "holy" in terms of our being set part as holy to Him. He does not always see our conduct as holy. We are already righteous and holy, but we are not yet fully righteous and holy.

That's why when Jesus speaks to the seven congregations in Asia Minor in Revelation 2–3, addressing each "angel" or leader, He starts with these words: "I know your works" (Rev 2:2, 9, 13, 19; 3:1, 8, 15). This is then followed by a specific critique of the things that were wrong in these congregations, along with specific praise for the things that were right, with words of promise and encouragement for those who would repent.

Jesus did *not* see these congregations (and their leaders) as perfectly holy and righteous, in which case there would have been no place for correction. Nor would He have said to them, "I know your works." But He *did* see them as declared righteous by God and called to be holy, because of which He rebuked some for failing to live this out and commended others for being faithful in their calling. (I'll return to Revelation 2–3 in chapter 11.)

The ministry school that I founded, FIRE School of Ministry, has specific requirements for our students, including moral and spiritual guidelines, and from the day we accept a student into the school until the day that person graduates, we ask that individual to abide by these standards. Most of the standards do not pertain to matters of salvation. For example, we have a total abstinence policy regarding alcohol, though we don't believe someone will go to hell for having a glass of wine. But because these are requirements for our school, even during summer breaks or even in the months leading up to their first class, we expect students to abide by these standards.

That means that if you get accepted to FIRE in March but classes don't start until August, we ask you to live as if you were already in the school. Because you have been accepted as a student, we want you to think of yourself as a FIRE student and conduct your life accordingly, even though you are still living at home, still not taking our classes, and still not on our campus enjoying all the advantages that come with the vibrant spiritual atmosphere there. You might even still be a senior in high school or a student at another college campus, yet we're asking you to live as a FIRE student even now.

That is a very poor analogy, but it is a picture of what "already but not yet" looks like, of what it means to have one foot in the world to come and one foot in this world, to be seated in heavenly places but still living here on earth, to be dead to sin but still dealing with sin.

Modern grace teachers have misunderstood these truths, as if the positional realities are the only realities, as if we are always perfectly holy and righteous in God's sight, as if there is no battle to fight with sin since we have already died to it. Because of this error, these teachers sometimes ridicule those who hold to a more biblically balanced position as if we were in some kind of spiritual Stone Age.

But rather than get into a spiritual war with those in error, let's focus on living out the truth. That will bring glory to God and gratification to our own souls.

Chapter 6

WHAT DOES IT MEAN TO BE UNDER GRACE AND NOT THE LAW?

I know there are commandments given to us in the New Testament, but why is this if we're not under law but under grace? What does it even mean to be under grace and not the law?

SOME MODERN TEACHERS explain grace by contrasting it with the law, which they see as bad. After all, one of the foundational truths of the New Testament is that in Jesus we are not under law but under grace (Rom. 6:14). Yet too often in their efforts to affirm grace, they throw out the baby with the bathwater. There is no problem with God's perfect and beautiful Law (Torah) or with His standards and rules. Indeed, the Apostle Paul was careful to point out that "the law is holy, and the commandment is holy and just and good" (Rom. 7:12). The problem is with our inability to keep God's law in our own power and strength.

"But," you may be thinking, "didn't Paul also say 'the power of sin is the law' and that Christ redeemed us from the curse of the law (1 Cor. 15:56, ESV; Gal. 3:13)? How, then, could the law be good?" Let me explain by first giving you some background.

In the Book of Jeremiah God told the people of Israel and Judah that although He was punishing them for their many sins, in the future He would make a new covenant with them. He said it would not be like the Sinai covenant (Exod. 19–24), which they broke and because of which He judged them severely, sending them into exile. Instead, it would be a better covenant, one in which He would forgive their sins and remember those sins no more. Under this new covenant His law (or laws) would be written on His people's hearts. They would now obey Him automatically, by nature, not even needing a teacher to tell them they should know the Lord and serve Him. (See Jeremiah 31:31–34.)

So important was this prophecy that it is repeated twice in Hebrews, once in the eighth chapter and once in the tenth chapter. In fact, it was so important that it is quoted in full in Hebrews 8 (vv. 8–12), representing the longest passage from the Old Testament quoted in the New Testament. The very notion of a "new testament" goes back to this wonderful prophetic word, and as Jewish and Gentile followers of the

Messiah of Israel, we enjoy the firstfruits of this new and better covenant.

God has forgiven our sins once and for all, and He remembers them no more. (See chapter 2.) And rather than having to submit to a set of external regulations that are written on stone (while our hearts remain like stone), God gives us a new heart and writes His laws on our hearts. It becomes our true nature to love Him, serve, and obey Him. (See Ezekiel 36:26–27.) We are new creations in the Messiah (2 Cor. 5:17) from the inside out. That is the power of God's grace.

What, then, does Paul mean when he writes in Romans 6:14 that we are not under law but under grace? The context makes it 100 percent clear that he is not saying that we can sin as much as we want because we are not under the law but under grace; or that, worse still, we *should* sin more so that God would show His grace even more.

Paul countered that bizarre way of thinking in the beginning of the chapter, writing, "What shall we say then? Are we to continue in sin that grace may abound? By no means! How can we who died to sin still live in it?" (Rom. 6:1–2, ESV). Where would anyone get such a strange idea? Well, Paul had just finished explaining how Adam's sin brought the curse of death on the whole human race, but he continued, "Where sin increased, grace abounded much more, so that just as sin reigned in death, grace might reign through righteousness unto eternal life through Jesus Christ our Lord" (Rom. 5:20–21).

Could it be, then, if we continue to sin, God will continue to show more and more grace? Perish the thought, says Paul. In Jesus we have died to sin. How can we continue to live in it? And that is the theme of the rest of Romans 6. He explains that through water baptism we have died to sin and have risen up in new life in Jesus, just as Jesus died and rose, and we are now united in a new life in Him.

In short, "We know that our old self was crucified with him in order that the body of sin might be brought to nothing, so that we would no longer be enslaved to sin" (Rom. 6:6, ESV). But this spiritual reality must be grasped: "You also must consider yourselves dead to sin and alive to God in Christ Jesus. Let not sin therefore reign in your mortal body, to make you obey its passions" (Rom. 6:11–12, ESV).

Paul is urging us to renew our minds and take hold of the fact that in Jesus we have died to sin, we have been freed from sin, and we have been empowered to live for God. Sin is still there, and there is a battle in our flesh, but we must not let sin dominate. He writes, "Do not yield your members to sin as instruments of unrighteousness, but yield yourselves to God, as those who are alive from the dead, and your bodies to God as instruments of righteousness. For sin shall not have dominion over you, for you are not under the law, but under grace" (vv. 13–14).

Do you grasp what Paul is saying? When we were under law, we were constantly reminded of our failures and shortcomings as we acknowledged that God's laws were good but failed to keep those laws, having to repeat an annual cycle of repentance and atonement to come into right relationship with Him. The Sinai system of the old covenant condemned us, not because God's holy laws were defective but because we were defective. We are no longer under that system!

That's also what Paul meant when he wrote, "The sting of death is sin, and the power of sin is the law" (1 Cor. 15:56, ESV). God made the Sinai covenant with Israel, and Israel failed under it, just as any other nation would have done, since we cannot live up to God's laws without His supernatural help. And the more we are told not to sin, the more we sin, since our sinful desires are awakened by the command not to sin.

DON'T TOUCH!

This is similar to the sign on a wall that says, "Don't touch. Wet paint." Suddenly you want to touch that wall, even though you never once thought of touching it before. The command "Don't touch" makes you want to touch. That's how it is with us, but on a much deeper level. And so, as soon as God gave His Ten Commandments to His people—these are all wonderful commandments—His people disobeyed those very commandments. To repeat: "The power of sin is the law," and we are not under law but under grace.

Naturally some would misunderstand that truth and think, "Then I guess I can do whatever I want!" And so Paul counters that erroneous way of thinking for the second time in Romans 6, writing:

> What then? Shall we sin because we are not under the law but under grace? God forbid! Do you not know that to whom you yield yourselves as slaves to obey, you are slaves of the one whom you obey, whether of sin leading to death, or of obedience leading to righteousness? But thanks be to God, for you were slaves of sin, but you have obeyed from the heart that form of teaching to which you were entrusted, and having been freed from sin, you became the slaves of righteousness.
> —ROMANS 6:15–18

So Paul's point is that we are no longer part of a system that showed us what was right but didn't empower us to do what was right, a system that commanded us to obey and then condemned us for disobeying, a system that didn't save us but rather was intended to show us our need for a Savior. We are no longer under the old system (the law as expressed through the Sinai covenant) but under a new system (grace as expressed through the death and resurrection of Jesus). In and through Jesus we have now died to sin and been raised up to lead a new life—a life of holiness and purity, a life of obedience and submission, a life where God's laws are now written on our hearts (Rom. 2:15), a life where our bodies become temples of the Spirit and God makes His dwelling among us (2 Cor. 6:16–19).

Our lives are still marked by divine commandments: Jesus said if we love Him, we will keep His commandments (John 14:15, 23), and John wrote that "this is the love of God, that we keep His commandments. And His commandments are not burdensome" (1 John 5:3).

As we spend time in God's presence in union with Jesus, we find that it is our heart's desire to keep the commandments of God. After all, they are the way of life!

So, being "under grace, not law" doesn't mean the Lord doesn't give us instructions and commands—the entire New Testament is filled with these instructions and commands—and it doesn't mean we can't displease the Lord or grieve Him (quite the contrary). But it does mean we are no longer under the condemnation of the law, we are no longer under the law as a system of justification and righteousness, and we are no longer under the law as a protector and guide that will lead us to the Messiah. (See Galatians 3:24–25. The Greek speaks of Israel being under a pedagogue, meaning the Sinai covenant, before the Messiah came.)

We have become sons and daughters of God on a personal and individual level, our sins have been blotted out, and our internal nature has been changed. There is still a battle we must fight as long as we live in this world. To quote Peter,

"Beloved, I urge you as sojourners and exiles to abstain from the passions of the flesh, which wage war against your soul" (1 Pet. 2:11, ESV).

But as we once were slaves of sin, we are now slaves of righteousness, and that is the reality we must wrap our minds around. The Spirit of God lives in us, and by His power we can live radically new lives. That is the power of grace!

As expressed in the old poem:

> To run and work the law commands,
> Yet gives me neither feet nor hands;
> But better news the gospel brings;
> It bids me fly and gives me wings.[1]

Go ahead and fly! That is the power of grace.

Chapter 7

IF GOD REQUIRES ANYTHING OF US AS BELIEVERS, HOW IS THAT GRACE?

I've heard that if I think God requires anything of me as a believer, then I'm mixing law with grace and I'm working for my salvation. Self-effort seems to be the opposite of grace.

PART OF THE hyper-grace message is that we aren't supposed to strive or work at being spiritual. "Jesus already paid the price," they say, "and all you have to do is accept it. There's no way you can add to what He's done for you, and if you try to do so, you are mixing faith with works or grace with law. All you need to *do* is let the Lord do His work through you."

Some of this message is wonderfully true, but there are other parts that are not true—actually, there are parts that are missing, and those missing parts can prove fatal.

It is true that salvation is a free gift and there's nothing we can do to earn it. God forgives us and saves us based on His goodness, not our goodness, merit, efforts, hard work, or sacrifice. Jesus paid for our salvation in full on the cross, and we can only receive it as a gift, not as something earned. The New Testament is quite clear on that (Rom. 3:28; 9:31–32; Eph. 2:8–9; 2 Tim. 1:9; Titus 3:5, just to name a few).

At the same time, the New Testament is equally clear that when we are saved—when our sins are forgiven and we become children of God—we belong to the Lord, and our life's purpose is now to do His will. That's why we call Him Lord: He is not just our friend, Savior, helper, and big brother. He is also our God, our King, and our Master. He is our Lord, and we belong to Him—literally. The Scriptures even tell us He bought us and actually owns us.

> Flee from sexual immorality. Every other sin a person commits is outside the body, but the sexually immoral person sins against his own body. Or do you not know that your body is a temple of the Holy Spirit within you, whom you have from God? *You are not your own, for you were bought with a price.* So glorify God in your body.
> —1 Corinthians 6:18–20, esv,
> emphasis added

> *You were bought with a price*; do not become bondservants of men.
> —1 CORINTHIANS 7:23, ESV,
> EMPHASIS ADDED

Is there any doubt about what Paul is saying here? And these are just two passages out of scores that could be quoted, each of which details what our Father requires of us as His children.

Put another way, now that we're in God's family, He expects us to live as His children. That's why throughout the New Testament we are given directives, commandments, and exhortations all based on our high calling—we are now sons and daughters of almighty God!— and on the price that was paid for our salvation. As Paul expressed it clearly and concisely, "Therefore I, a prisoner for serving the Lord, beg you to lead a life worthy of your calling, for you have been called by God" (Eph. 4:1, NLT).

You might ask, "But how is this grace?" Perhaps you are misunderstanding grace. Perhaps someone has given you a wrong definition of grace, claiming that if God requires anything of you under grace, then it is no longer grace. Where is that written in the Bible?

It is not grace if we have to work for our salvation; it is certainly grace if God calls us to walk worthy of that salvation and then empowers us by that same grace to do so.

Let me give you a simple illustration. Imagine that you were poorly educated and really bad in math. One day you get a call from the biggest accounting firm in your city. They want to give you a job, and they will train you at their expense, however long it takes. They are going to make you into the best, most well-paid accountant in the region! They're also going to buy you a brand-new wardrobe, since everyone in the company is required to dress well, and they're going to send a limo to pick you up every morning at 8:00 a.m. to begin the training. What's more, they will start paying you five thousand dollars a week while you train.

You don't deserve it—in fact, you are totally unworthy—and everything they're doing for you is based on their generosity, not your merit. In that sense, it is all based on grace. At the same time, they require you to put on the new clothes they bought you, to be ready when the limo picks you up in the morning, and to go through the training process every day. That is what the company requires of its employees, and now that you are one of the employees—by grace!—you are expected to comply, all with their help, every step of the way. You are not earning the company's benefits; you are simply doing what the company requires in response to their gracious actions toward you.

"But," you say, "I'm not God's employee. I'm God's child. There's quite a difference between the two."

Actually, the Scriptures tell us that we are sons of God relationally and servants of God vocationally. That's why Paul explained to the Corinthians that the believer who is free (meaning not a slave owned by someone) is now "Christ's slave" (1 Cor. 7:22, NIV), and that's why Paul, Peter, Jacob (James), and Jude identified themselves as servants (a word that actually means a slave or bondservant in the Greek) of the Lord. (See, for example, Romans 1:1; Jacob [James] 1:1; 2 Peter 1:1; Jude 1:1.) As stated before, we have been bought with a price and we now belong to the Lord, and there is no better place to be than in the service of God.

That being said, we'll switch from the "employee" analogy and focus instead on being a child of God. Let's say you're a pauper living on the streets, freezing in the cold at night and starving for food during the day, eating out of garbage cans just to survive. One day the king of your country sends a personal entourage for you, and to your total shock, you are informed that the king is adopting you as his own child and that you will now live as royalty in the palace with the king's family.

You are also given an amazing new set of clothes—like nothing else you've ever seen— along with the most expensive watch on the planet and the finest jewels. As for your room, it's bigger than most people's houses, and it's all yours and yours alone. Who could ever dream of anything like that? And when you ask the king why he chose you, he explains that he wanted to show his love and goodness to the most undeserving subject in his kingdom, and that subject was you. What amazing grace!

Then he tells you, "Now that you are royalty, you are expected to live like royalty, and that means getting rid of your old pauper's clothes, taking a bath every day, wearing a new set of clothes for the royal meals, and keeping your room tidy. My royal staff will assist you in doing this every day."

All this has nothing to do with earning a place in the king's family—you could never do that— nor is it mixing grace and works (to put it in spiritual terms). It is simply what is expected of royalty. In the same way, now that we are children of God—totally by grace—we are called to live like children of God.

This is taught throughout the New Testament, where the Lord calls us to walk worthy of His grace (Eph. 4:1; Col. 1:10; 1 Thess. 2:12). That means that if we say God requires nothing of us under grace, *we are misrepresenting grace.* Grace comes with both responsibility and accountability.

You might say, "Then it's no longer grace. If there's anything I can do to impact my relationship with God in a negative way, that's salvation by works, not grace."

Actually that is not what the Bible says, and it is the Bible that defines grace for us, not a contemporary teacher (including me). God clearly calls us to walk worthy of the grace He has poured out on us, and He makes clear that we can please or displease Him by our actions, words, and thoughts. (For more on the question of pleasing God, see chapter 11.)

Read again the words of Paul. I certainly believe he understood grace! In light of God's grace, he called on his readers to walk worthy of their lofty spiritual standing:

> Only let your conduct be *worthy of the gospel of Christ.*
> —Philippians 1:27,
> emphasis added

For this reason we also, since the day we heard it [about your faith], do not cease to pray for you and to ask that you may be filled with the knowledge of His will in all wisdom and spiritual understanding; that you may *walk in a manner worthy of the Lord*, pleasing to all, being fruitful in every good work, and increasing in the knowledge of God.

—Colossians 1:9–10,

emphasis added

We exhorted each one of you and encouraged you and charged you to walk in a manner *worthy of God*, who calls you into his own kingdom and glory.

—1 Thessalonians 2:12, esv,

emphasis added

We are now members of Christ's very body and branches of His life-giving vine, serving as His ambassadors and representatives in this world. It should be no surprise that we must live worthy of the One whom we represent.

You might ask, "Then what's the difference between an old covenant believer and a new covenant believer, between a believer under the Sinai covenant and a believer under grace? If God requires works from both, where is the grace?"

That is an important question, so let's break it down into two parts, addressing the second part of your question first.

GOOD WORKS ARE THE FRUIT OF OUR FAITH

What is the place of good works in the New Testament under grace? According to the universal testimony of all New Testament writers, our good works are the proof and fruit of our faith.

Paul preached to both Jews and Gentiles that they "should repent and turn to God and do works proving their repentance" (Acts 26:20). And in one of his greatest expositions of grace in the Bible (Eph. 2:1–10) he wrote, "For by grace you have been saved through faith, and this is not of yourselves. It is the gift of God, not of works, so that no one should boast. For we are His workmanship, created in Christ Jesus for good works, which God prepared beforehand, so that we should walk in them" (vv. 8–10). Grace and works go hand in hand, with our good works being the natural expression of God's gracious work in our lives.

In keeping with this teaching, Paul wrote to Titus:

> For the grace of God that brings salvation has appeared to all men, teaching us that, denying ungodliness and worldly desires, we should live soberly, righteously, and in godliness in this present world, as we await the blessed hope and the appearing of the glory of our great God and Savior Jesus Christ, who gave Himself for us, that He might redeem us from all lawlessness and purify for Himself a special people, zealous of good works.
> —Titus 2:11–14

There you have it again: grace results in good works, which is why Paul urged Titus to remind his hearers "to be submissive to rulers and authorities, to be obedient, to be ready for every good work" (Titus 3:1, ESV). A person can teach grace and call on God's people to live godly lives and do good works. It is not either-or; it is both-and.

Jacob (James) confirmed this as well, writing:

> What good is it, dear brothers and sisters, if you say you have faith but don't show it by your actions? Can that kind of faith save anyone? Suppose you see a brother or sister who has no food or clothing, and you say, "Good-bye and have a good day; stay warm and eat well"—but then you don't give that person any food or clothing. What good does that do? So you see, faith by itself isn't enough. Unless it produces good deeds, it is dead and useless. Now someone may argue, "Some people have faith; others have good deeds." But I say, "How can you show me your faith if you

don't have good deeds? I will show you
my faith by my good deeds."
—JAMES 2:14–18, NLT

Now, returning to the first part of this chapter's question, how is this different from the
Sinai covenant? There are actually many pronounced differences between life under the Sinai
covenant and life under the new covenant:

- Under the Sinai covenant there
  were perpetual sacrifices for our
  sins; under the new covenant there
  was one, once-for-all sacrifice made.

- Under the Sinai covenant righteousness came by the deeds of the
  Law; under the new covenant righteousness comes by faith in the
  Messiah.

- Under the Sinai covenant God
  spoke with terrifying fire in the
  midst of a dark cloud; under the

new covenant He speaks to us face-
to-face through His Son.

- Under the Sinai covenant only the
  high priest could enter the holiest
  place (the holy of holies in the tab-
  ernacle or temple); under the new
  covenant every believer has direct
  access to the holy of holies in
  heaven.

- Under the Sinai covenant there
  were blessings for obedience and
  curses for disobedience; under the
  new covenant we begin with every
  spiritual blessing in Christ stored
  up for us in heaven.

But this is what is so fascinating. According
to Hebrews, because we have been given so
much under the new and better covenant—
that's a major theme of the book—much more is
required from us. Can I share with you what the
author of Hebrews wrote? It is clear that he had
quite a grasp on the meaning of grace as well:

Therefore we must pay much closer attention to what we have heard, lest we drift away from it. For since the message declared by angels proved to be reliable, and every transgression or disobedience received a just retribution [he is speaking here of the Sinai covenant], how shall we escape if we neglect such a great salvation [he is speaking here about salvation by grace]? It was declared at first by the Lord, and it was attested to us by those who heard, while God also bore witness by signs and wonders and various miracles and by gifts of the Holy Spirit distributed according to his will.

—Hebrews 2:1–4, esv

Exhortations like this are found throughout Hebrews, including these strong words from Hebrews 10. Will you read them prayerfully, asking God to make these verses real to you?

Anyone who despised Moses' law died without mercy in the presence of two or three witnesses. How much more severe a punishment do you suppose he deserves, who has trampled under foot the Son of God, and has regarded the blood of the covenant that sanctified him to be a common thing, and has insulted the Spirit of grace? For we know Him who said, "Vengeance is Mine," says the Lord, "I will repay." And again He says, "The Lord will judge His people." It is a fearful thing to fall into the hands of the living God.

—HEBREWS 10:28–31

Because so much has been given to us at such a high cost—the blood of God's own Son, not the blood of an animal sacrifice—much is required of us. Please don't call this "legalism" or "dead religion." To do so is to insult the Spirit of grace and to make light of the price God paid to save you and me. This is sacred stuff!

Hebrews addresses this once more in a remarkable passage that contrasts life under the Sinai covenant with life under the new covenant. You will be surprised by the application, which I will highlight in the text when we reach it.

First, the author of Hebrews describes what Israel experienced at Mount Sinai. It was terrifying indeed:

> You have not come to a mountain that can be touched and that burned with fire, and to blackness and darkness and storm, and to the sound of a trumpet and to a voice speaking words, such that those who heard them begged that the word not be spoken to them anymore. For they could not endure that which was commanded: "If so much as a beast touches the mountain, it must be stoned or thrust through with a spear." So terrible was the sight that Moses said, "I am terrified and trembling."
> —HEBREWS 12:18–21

Next, he contrasts that experience with our experience as believers under grace:

> But you have come to Mount Zion and to the city of the living God, the heavenly Jerusalem, and to an innumerable company of angels; to the general

assembly and church of the firstborn, who are enrolled in heaven; to God, the Judge of all; and to the spirits of the righteous ones made perfect; and to Jesus, the Mediator of a new covenant; and to the sprinkled blood that speaks better than that of Abel.

—HEBREWS 12:22–24

What an incredible difference!

Then he draws the conclusion, giving this exhortation: "See that you do not refuse Him who is speaking. For if they did not escape when they refused Him who spoke on earth, much less shall we escape if we turn away from Him who speaks from heaven" (Heb. 12:25).

Now, you might not like this, and it may not make you feel comfortable, but the goal of these words is not to comfort us; it is to make us sober. Don't play games with grace! (As for comfort, there are thousands of other verses that bring comfort and assurance, and we drink them in too.)

These verses from Hebrews also may not correspond with definitions of grace you have heard from some modern teachers. But rather than try to reinterpret the Bible to fit these definitions, it's best to derive our definitions from what the Bible actually says, not what we want it to say. Some of the worst interpretations of Scripture I've seen in my life come from hyper-grace teachers trying to squeeze the Word into their theology. Instead, let's allow the Word to form our theology, taking in the testimony of the whole Bible. Only then will we be on sure and solid ground.

So enjoy the amazing, incredible, almost indescribable depths of God's grace expressed through Jesus, and by that same grace walk worthy of your high calling in the Lord. Since we are God's own workmanship (Eph. 2:10; the New Living Translation actually says we are His "masterpiece"), let's live this out to the full. As Paul also wrote, "For at one time you were darkness, but now you are light in the Lord. Walk as children of light (for the fruit of light is found in all that is good and right and true), and try to discern what is pleasing to the Lord" (Eph. 5:8–10, ESV).

That really says it all. Let's walk as children of light!

Chapter 8

ARE WE MADE COMPLETELY HOLY THE MOMENT WE ARE SAVED?

I read in Hebrews 12:14 that without holiness, no one will see the Lord—and, frankly, that verse scares me. What if I'm not holy enough? Will I not see the Lord? My friends who embrace the modern grace message tell me that the moment I was born again, I was made completely holy, and they have encouraged me not to worry about trying to be more holy.

ONE OF THE most important—and controversial—issues that will arise as you explore the subject of grace is the question of sanctification (or our holiness). Modern grace teachers largely reject the idea that we are called to grow in holiness and that we must pursue holiness. They claim that the moment we were saved, we were made perfectly, totally, and forever holy in God's sight, regardless of what we do or how we live. So they say we were not only completely justified by faith, once and for all, but we were also completely sanctified by faith, once and for all.

Yet the Bible calls us to "pursue holiness," to "be holy," and to "be perfect," and speaks of us as presently "being sanctified." So what are we to make of this? It's really not too complicated.

According to the Bible, there are three phases to our holiness:

- Phase one: You are declared holy the moment you are forgiven, at which time God puts you in the

"holy, set apart" column. You are
now a saint!

- Phase two: As a saint—a holy one—
  you are called to grow in that identity and to be holy in your thoughts,
  words, and deeds. This is a require-
  ment, not an option. You are part
  of God's family, purchased with the
  blood of Jesus.

- Phase three: When you are resurrected, you will be made perfectly
  holy forever, never capable of sinning again and never desiring to sin
  again. That will be amazing!

We can see phase one in verses like
1 Corinthians 6:11, which says that *we have
already been sanctified*, meaning set apart as
holy to the Lord. This happened the moment we
were born again. We can see phase two in verses
like 1 Thessalonians 4:3, where Paul writes that
it is God's will be that we *be sanctified*, meaning
that we live holy lives before Him, which is our

lifelong calling. Phase three is found in verses like 1 John 3:2, which tells us that when Jesus appears at His second coming, we will become just like Him, which includes receiving our new resurrected bodies, bodies that will no longer be tempted to sin.

As far as whether we can grow in holiness as children of God, the entire New Testament answers this with a great big yes. It is part of our spiritual destiny to become more and more like Jesus in this world until we see Him face-to-face.

Unfortunately there is a lot of confusion about this subject in the church today. On the one side is the hyper-grace camp that tells you it is a "spiritually murderous lie" to teach that holiness is progressive, meaning that we are called to grow and progress in holiness.[1] On the other side is the legalistic camp that constantly tells you that you're a sinner and that if you don't improve your ways, you won't make it into heaven, which turns holiness into an external list of dos and don'ts. Both sides are wrong.

The hyper-grace teachers misunderstand phase two—that holiness is progressive—while the legalists misunderstand phase one—that we are made holy at salvation. Yet both phases are important for our self-identity and our walk in the Lord.

Practically speaking, if we misunderstand phase one, as legalists do, we will not find our identity as "holy ones," which is absolutely foundational. Just imagine how different life is for the person who says every day, "I'm just a sinner saved by grace," compared to the person who says, "I'm a saint—a holy one!—by God's grace!" At the same time, if we don't understand phase two, we will be resistant to calls to holy living, branding such calls "legalism" or "dead religion" or worse.

Let's take a journey through the New Testament scriptures, beginning with a fascinating verse in 1 Corinthians that addresses this issue directly and does so in just a few short words. Paul writes at the beginning of his letter, "To the church of God in Corinth, to those *sanctified* in Christ Jesus and called to be his *holy people*" (1 Cor. 1:2, NIV, emphasis added). Or, to translate the relevant words more literally to bring out what the Greek is saying, we might say, "To those *made holy* in Christ Jesus and *called to be holy.*" This sums things up well: the moment we put our faith in Jesus as Lord and Savior, He forgives our sins, puts us in right standing with God, and calls us holy—meaning separated to God and set apart from sin.

That's what the word *saints* means in most of our English translations, and it is found throughout the New Testament, including in other translations of 1 Corinthians 1:2. (See, for example, the English Standard Version's "to those sanctified in Christ Jesus, called to be saints," which is almost identical to many other Bible versions, including the King James.) The believers are called "saints" (holy ones!) in Acts (Acts 9:13, 32, 41; 26:10), in Romans (Rom. 8:27; 12:13; 15:25–26, 31; 16:2, 15; and in 1:7 we are "called to be saints"), and then several dozen times more in the other books of the New Testament. Paul even writes toward the end of some of his letters, "All the saints greet you" (2 Cor. 13:13; Phil. 4:22).

If you are a child of God, you are a saint—a holy one, a sanctified one—and that becomes a reality from the moment you become born again, even before you've had the opportunity to change your conduct. As Paul wrote to the Corinthians, after giving a list of sinful behaviors that will exclude people from God's kingdom, "And such were some of you. But you were washed, you were sanctified [meaning 'made holy'], you were justified in the name of the Lord Jesus Christ and by the Spirit of our God" (1 Cor. 6:11, ESV).

This is confirmed in Ephesians, where Paul tells us that in Jesus we have been "created after the likeness of God in true righteousness and holiness" (Eph. 4:24, ESV). See also 1 Corinthians 1:30, where Paul writes, "And because of him you are in Christ Jesus, who became to us wisdom from God, righteousness and sanctification and redemption" (ESV). Jesus Himself is our righteousness, our sanctification, and our redemption.

But that is the beginning, not the end, and for the rest of our lives on this earth we are called to be holy in our conduct (1 Pet. 1:15), to pursue holiness (Heb. 12:14), and to perfect holiness (2 Cor. 7:1). As Paul prayed in 1 Thessalonians 5:23, "May the very God of peace sanctify you completely. And I pray to God that your whole spirit, soul, and body be preserved blameless unto the coming of our Lord Jesus Christ." If we were already completely sanctified, there would be no reason for Paul to pray like this. And to be completely candid, hyper-grace teachers who try to reinterpret this prayer to fit their theology do a real hatchet job on it. The prayer means what it says, and the Greek says clearly that our sanctification is not yet complete.

But Paul not only prayed for the Thessalonians, but he also gave them practical and firm instructions. As he wrote in 1 Thessalonians 4:3, "For this is the will of God, your sanctification..." Or, as stated in the New Living Translation, "God's will is for you to be holy."

What does that mean in our everyday lives? Paul lays it out simply and clearly:

> God's will is for you to be holy, so stay away from all sexual sin. Then each of you will control his own body and live in holiness and honor—not in lustful passion like the pagans who do not know God and his ways. Never harm or cheat a fellow believer in this matter by violating his wife, for the Lord avenges all such sins, as we have solemnly warned you before. God has called us to live holy lives, not impure lives. Therefore, anyone who refuses to live by these rules is not disobeying human teaching but is rejecting God, who gives his Holy Spirit to you.
>
> —1 THESSALONIANS 4:3–8, NLT

Being holy is not just a concept or spiritual state. It refers to how we live in this world, which is why many passages throughout the Bible make clear that our God, who Himself is holy, requires His children to be holy as well. And so, when we become His children through faith in His Son, God puts us in the "holy" column and calls us "holy ones" (saints). Over the course of the rest of our lives He calls us to live that holiness out, based on the new nature He has given and based on His Spirit living within us, empowering us to be holy.

AM I HOLY ENOUGH?

"But I'm still confused," you might say. "How do I know if I'm holy enough? I could never be holy like God is."

That's a fair question, and what you're really asking is: "What if I have lustful thoughts once a month—is that too much? What about once a week? What about once a day? What if I'm not kind to my neighbor? How long do I have to fix that before God rejects me? What if I die on a day when I wasn't nice to my neighbor? Do I go to hell?"

Here's the simple answer: Jesus makes you holy enough to see God the moment you are born again. In that instant your sins are wiped way, your guilt is gone, and you have become a holy child of God. As explained in previous chapters, this is the amazing wonder of salvation. What a gift, what grace, what mercy!

Now, if you want to please the Lord and live in harmony with Him, you will seek to live a holy life, becoming more and more like Jesus in thought, word, and deed. That is the ultimate expression of holiness: becoming like Jesus. Who among us doesn't have that as our greatest goal and desire? Who among us doesn't want to be more like Him in every way? This is how we bear fruit proving our repentance (Acts 26:20): by demonstrating our faith through a changed life. As revival scholar James Edwin Orr said, "The only evidence of the new birth is the new life."[2]

But there's more: if you reject holiness and choose sin, refusing to repent and hardening your heart against God, then it is not just holiness you are rejecting; you are rejecting God Himself. As we read in 1 Thessalonians 4: "For God has not called us for impurity, but in holiness. Therefore whoever disregards this, disregards not man but

God, who gives his Holy Spirit to you" (1 Thess. 4:7–8, ESV).

This is similar to what is written in Hebrews 12:

> Strive for peace with everyone, and for the holiness without which no one will see the Lord. See to it that no one fails to obtain the grace of God; that no "root of bitterness" springs up and causes trouble, and by it many become defiled; that no one is sexually immoral or unholy like Esau, who sold his birthright for a single meal. For you know that afterward, when he desired to inherit the blessing, he was rejected, for he found no chance to repent, though he sought it with tears.
>
> —HEBREWS 12:14–17, ESV

We strive to live at peace with everyone and we strive to live holy lives, all with God's help and grace, recognizing the importance of holiness: no one will see God without it! And we are careful not to give ourselves over to sinful living, knowing the deadly consequences of sin. But we do this as saints—in the language of Hebrews, drawing near to God "with a true heart in full assurance of faith, having our hearts sprinkled to cleanse them from an evil conscience, and our bodies washed with pure water" (Heb. 10:22).

We do this as people who have been made holy by God and are now seeking to walk that holiness out in every area of life: in the way we treat our spouses and kids, in the way we respond to fleshly desires, in the way we react to those who are unlovely, in the attitudes we cultivate in our hearts, and in the words we speak to others. Pursuing and cultivating holiness is a beautiful thing!

How then do you feel secure in Jesus? By looking to the Cross, at what He did to purchase our salvation. He really did pay the full price!

How do you maintain solid fellowship with the Lord? By seeking to please Him in your daily life and by being quick to repent when you fall short.

What should cause you concern as a believer? If you are refusing God's grace and choosing disobedience, rejecting the lordship of Jesus, saying yes to the flesh and no to Him. When this becomes the pattern of your life—not just a momentary lapse—God gives you warnings rather than comfort. So turn back before it's too late.

When you do turn back, our Father will welcome you with open arms and give you a fresh, new start, overwhelming you with His mercy. The blood of the Cross will be freshly applied, and your heart will sing for you.

But He will not ignore our willful, unrepentant sin, which is why the New Testament contains many warnings against leaving the way of salvation. (See, for example, 2 Peter 2:20–22, which speaks of teachers who once knew the Lord but chose corruption instead.) In short, you are totally, 100 percent safe and secure in Christ unless you choose to leave that place of safety and security.

As for our many shortcomings and failings, which God knows infinitely better than we do, we need not fear. The Lord will finish the good work He started in us (Phil. 1:6), and on a daily basis we have the extraordinary privilege of partnering with Him to become more and more like His Son. What an incredible journey!

This is the beauty of 2 Corinthians 7:1, which I'll put in context before quoting it. Beginning in 2 Corinthians 6:14, Paul exhorts the believers to be separated from the sin of the world and from camaraderie with the devil, reminding them in 2 Corinthians 6:16 that they are temples of the living God. That means God Himself lives in our midst, because of which Paul exhorts us to come out from the pollution of the world and be separated. After all, we are God's people, God's children. In light of this, he writes in 2 Corinthians 7:1, "Therefore, since we have these promises, dear friends, let us purify ourselves from everything that contaminates body and spirit, perfecting holiness out of reverence for God" (NIV).

Because God has become our Father and has given us such precious promises—as the body of Christ we are now the temple He lives in, and as individual believers our bodies are temples of the Holy Spirit—we are called to purify our-selves and bring holiness to perfection in our lives. What a beautiful, sacred calling! What a precious invitation! Destined to be more beau-tiful than a bride in her pristine white wed-ding gown, we are called to keep ourselves free from things that contaminate our bodies and our spirits—meaning sin *can* contaminate a believer—"bringing holiness to completion in the fear of God" (2 Cor. 7:1, ESV).

I'm encouraging you—really, the Lord is encouraging you—not to look at holiness as some terrible burden but rather to view it as a wonderful invitation. Every day of our lives we can become more beautiful and less ugly, more spiritual and less fleshly, more like Jesus and less like the world. We don't need to play in the filthy pigpen of disobedience and sin. We can take on wings and fly into God's presence, resembling Him more and more as the years go on.

As 2 Peter tells us, "His divine power has granted to us all things that pertain to life and godliness, through the knowledge of him who called us to his own glory and excellence, by which he has granted to us his precious and very great promises, so that through them you may become partakers of the divine nature, having escaped from the corruption that is in the world because of sinful desire" (2 Pet. 1:3–4, ESV).

Peter continues:

> For this very reason, make every effort to supplement your faith with virtue, and virtue with knowledge, and knowledge with self-control, and self-control with steadfastness, and steadfastness with godliness, and godliness with brotherly affection, and brotherly affection with love. For if these qualities are yours and are increasing, they keep you from being ineffective or unfruitful in the knowledge of our Lord Jesus Christ. For whoever lacks these qualities is so nearsighted that he is blind, having forgotten that he was cleansed from his former sins. Therefore, brothers, be all the more diligent to confirm your

calling and election, for if you practice
these qualities you will never fall.

—2 Peter 1:5–10, esv

This is similar to what Peter wrote in his first
letter about the incredible salvation we have
received through Jesus:

Therefore, preparing your minds for
action, and being sober-minded, set
your hope fully on the grace that will be
brought to you at the revelation of Jesus
Christ. As obedient children, do not
be conformed to the passions of your
former ignorance, but as he who called
you is holy, you also be holy in all your
conduct, since it is written, "You shall
be holy, for I am holy." And if you call
on him as Father who judges impartially
according to each one's deeds, conduct
yourselves with fear throughout the time
of your exile, knowing that you were
ransomed from the futile ways inher-
ited from your forefathers, not with per-
ishable things such as silver or gold, but

with the precious blood of Christ, like
that of a lamb without blemish or spot.
—1 PETER 1:13–19, ESV

Paul states this very same thing in many passages, explaining in Romans 6 that since we have
died with Jesus, we must now live out our new
life in Him. "For just as you once presented your
members as slaves to impurity and to lawlessness leading to more lawlessness, so now present
your members as slaves to righteousness leading
to sanctification [holiness]" (Rom. 6:19, ESV).
Similarly, in Colossians 3 Paul writes that as
those who have died to our old lives and are now
sitting in heavenly places with Jesus, we should
put to death everything from that old life—from
sexual sin to anger—clothing ourselves with
God's love (Col. 3:1–14).

So also in Ephesians 4, where Paul stated that
through the new birth we had been created in
God's holy likeness, he told the Ephesians what
this meant in everyday life: put away falsehood
and anger; don't steal; speak only words that
build up others; don't grieve the Holy Spirit; get

rid of bitterness and wrath and be kind to each other; imitate the example of Jesus; walk and live as children of light (Eph. 4:20–5:12).

This is what holiness looks like, and it is our sacred calling as obedient children, our response to grace while also empowered by grace. It is also our sacred responsibility.

Let us then pursue holiness with joy and faith as well as with sobriety, seeking to be more and more like Jesus every day, spending quality time with Him so His qualities "rub off" on us all the more. This is who we are!

On April 7, 2006, I wrote this prayer in my journal: "Father, strike at the root of everything unclean in me, everything displeasing in me, everything in my nature that endures and persists that is contrary to Your nature. Strike it dead at the root, and show me how to walk this out for the rest of my life in ever-increasing holiness, purity, and devotion. I trust Your grace! I trust the power of the blood of Jesus!"

I encourage you to pray similar prayers in your own life, not in a self-condemning way—in

Jesus you are not condemned—but in a life-giving way, asking the Lord to help you uproot from the garden of your life everything that is not like Him.

This will be our blessed, lifelong pursuit—the pursuit of holiness. It's what holy ones do, and in Jesus we have been made holy. Let's live it out to the full until we see Him face-to-face.

Chapter 9

IF "HYPER-GRACE" TEACHING IS NOT TRUE, WHY ARE SO MANY BELIEVERS TRANSFORMED BY THE MESSAGE?

Many of my friends tell me they are closer to the Lord than they've ever been because of the so-called hyper-grace message, while others tell me to beware of this teaching. How can a bad message do so much good?

J ESUS MADE IT clear that a good tree cannot produce bad fruit, nor can a bad tree produce good fruit (Luke 6:43–44). It would follow, then, that since thousands of people have been positively affected by what I and others have called "hyper-grace" teaching, then that message must be sound, scriptural, and from the Lord. On the other hand, there are thousands of people who have been negatively affected by this same message, which would lead to the opposite conclusion. How can both be true at the same time? Wouldn't this contradict what Jesus said about trees and their fruit?

Not at all. Instead, we need to understand why some are helped and some are hurt, and we need to discern which parts of the message are true and which are false. Let me explain.

It appears that there are two primary types of believers drawn to the modern grace message. The first group consists of serious Christians who really want to please the Lord but struggle with a particular sin or have very sensitive consciences and always feel like they're falling short. They are not looking for a license to sin. They want to live godly lives, but they can't seem to find a place of freedom from sinful habits or a place of acceptance in the sight of God.

When they hear that all their sins are forgiven—past, present, and future—and that nothing they do can ever affect their relationship with God, and when they are taught that on the very worst day of their lives God sees them as perfect and holy, they take their eyes off themselves—off their performance and their failures and fix their eyes on Jesus. And as they do, they are wonderfully set free and transformed.

Was there a mixture of truth and error in what they heard? Without a doubt. But since they were not looking for an excuse to disobey or backslide, and since one of their biggest problems was measuring their relationship with God on the basis of how they performed on a given day, the exaggerated message of grace was liberating for them.

On the other hand, there are believers who are attracted to the hyper-grace message because they have a problem with discipline and holiness. When they listen to these same hyper-grace sermons, they become complacent, carnal, and compromised, mocking those who call for holy living, branding them grace-hating Pharisees, and claiming that they are mixing grace with works. Rather than draw closer to the Lord in intimate prayer, consistent reading of the Word, and deepening purity, they actually backslide in the name of grace.

So then, the positive truths of the modern grace message, even in exaggerated form, are incredibly liberating when received by those who want to please the Lord. But the exaggerations, distortions, and errors are also deadly and destructive, especially for those who are looking for a way to accommodate the flesh rather than crucify it.

I'm sure many believers are drawn to the hyper-grace message because they have been burned by legalism, but the problem is that they often swing from one extreme to the other, going from one form of deception to another form of deception. Why not move from error to truth?

To repeat: it is the true parts of the modern grace message that are helping millions of people around the world, and all of us should proclaim these truths as loudly and clearly as possible. They include the teaching that:

- We should put our focus on Jesus and not on ourselves.

- Salvation is a free gift that we could never earn in a million lifetimes.

- On the worst day of our lives God deeply loves us.

- Committing one sin does not cause us to lose our salvation.

- If we fail to confess a sin, that doesn't mean we are not saved.

- Even if we commit a sin, as far as our salvation is concerned, we are still in the "forgiven" column.

- We are still God's children, even as we struggle with sin.

- The moment we are saved, God sets us apart as holy and even calls us holy.

- God's grace empowers us to live above sin.

- The Holy Spirit is not here to condemn us.

- Holiness is not a matter of keeping a set of external laws.

It's a shame that many pastors and leaders sometimes fail to emphasize these truths, because of which a new "grace revolution" rises up every few decades to bring balance. Unfortunately it often goes way too far, mixing truth with error to the point that others have to counterbalance the hyper-grace message with a more biblically based version of grace.

Let me give you an illustration to show how an exaggerated message of grace can still help many people despite the errors it contains. Let's say you love Jesus, but due to wrong teaching or your own temperament you live in daily fear that you will backslide, deny the Lord, and go to hell. Because of that tormenting fear, you are super-conscious of every sin you commit, down to the tiniest detail, feeling that you have to confess every single sin before you fall asleep at night in order to "stay saved." You end up living with so much self-condemnation that you find it hard to pray, read the Word, or go to church services—"After all," you say to yourself, "why would God want to spend time with a wretched person like me?" And the more you focus on your sins, the more you seem to commit them.

Then one day you turn on the TV and hear a preacher with Bible in hand, going through the Scriptures and teaching on grace. He tells you that the moment you were saved, all your sins were pronounced forgiven, even the ones you have not yet committed. He tells you that you never need to confess your sins again to receive forgiveness and that the Holy Spirit will never convict you of your sins. Best of all, he tells you that in God's sight you already made it, that you are saved forever and cannot possibly lose your salvation, and that God loves you 24/7 with a perfect love, even on your most sinful day.

Suddenly the sun starts shining in your dark life, and all you want to do is pray and read the Word and share the gospel with others. "What a wonderful Savior!" you say. "I am truly saved! I am truly loved!"

Truth Mixed With Error

The problem, of course, is that there is truth mixed with error in the message you heard on TV, and that error could open the door to sin in the future. And as you continue to study the Word, you will encounter verses that contradict parts of the message. At that point you will either get confused, start reinterpreting the Word based on your understanding of grace, get fed up and walk away from the Lord, or in the best-case scenario, embrace biblical grace rather than hyper-grace.

If you embrace biblical grace, you will still realize that God's desire is to bless you, care for you, and spend eternity with you; that His love is still fixed on you, even when you sin; that confession of sin as a believer is for the purpose of relationship, not salvation; that you never have to fear losing your salvation if you have truly committed your life to the Lord; that the Holy Spirit convicts but doesn't condemn; and that His conviction is designed to bring you near to the Father, not drive you away.

All this means that we can approach the throne of God with total confidence, "in full assurance of faith, having our hearts sprinkled to cleanse them from an evil conscience, and our bodies washed with pure water" (Heb. 10:22). And we can do this without the message of hyper-grace. But you can readily see how a true message with serious error can still help certain people.

Let me also give you an illustration that is natural rather than spiritual. Imagine a gifted athlete who strove so much for perfection and feared failure so acutely that she could never perform to her full potential. Because she was so tense, she could not just let her gifts and training take over. She began to meet with a sports psychologist who convinced her that she was going to win an Olympic medal and that she should take the pressure off herself and instead just enjoy her sport. And so, lifted in her spirits, she rose up to her full potential and dominated her sport.

What's the point of the story? A positive attitude helped this athlete, leading to victories, but the positive attitude was based on the assurance of future victories, even though no such assurance was factually available at the time.

To be clear, my illustration is *not* intended as a direct parallel to the modern grace message in terms of the content of the respective messages. What *is* intended is the point that a message not entirely based on definite, ascertainable truth can produce a very positive result because of the good content it contains. And that is how it is with hyper-grace. So as the old saying goes, eat the meat but spit out the bones.

You might say, "But I feel like you really want me to spit out the meat—the very heart and soul of the grace message—since the things that have really helped me are the things you say are in error."

Actually, you can rest 100 percent secure in your relationship with Jesus without believing in the "once saved, always saved" doctrine. And you can enjoy the favor and smile of God 24/7 without believing that it is impossible to displease Him. You can also live totally free from condemnation without believing that the Holy Spirit will never convict you of your sins, and you can walk in assurance of forgiveness without believing that confession of sin is not for believers. I'm a living witness to these realities, as are countless millions of believers worldwide.

The key, then, is to get rid of false and unbiblical thinking and to renew our minds and hearts with the truths of God's Word—liberating truths, life-giving truths, transforming truths—rather than to fill our minds with lots of wonderful truth mixed with some very dangerous error. But we must be very careful not to react against hyper-grace teaching to the point that we develop a bad attitude toward grace. God forbid!

Instead, let us appreciate the emphasis put on grace by these modern grace teachers, even if it is an overemphasis, asking our Father to open our hearts to the fullness of the revelation of His grace expressed toward us in Jesus. And let us appreciate the emphasis that these teachers put on the Son of God, recognizing that in all things He must be preeminent (Col. 1:13–20). It is by focusing on Him and drawing our life from Him that we demonstrate to a dying world what this new life is all about. Indeed, "[the Son] is the brightness of [God's] glory, the express image of Himself, and upholds all things by the word of His power. When He had by Himself purged our sins, He sat down at the right hand of the Majesty on high" (Heb. 1:3).

When we look to Him, we will never be disappointed. But looking to Him also means listening to Him, which is why it is so important that we do not ignore the words that Jesus spoke. We'll take that up in the next chapter.

Chapter 10

DO THE WORDS OF JESUS APPLY TO US TODAY?

I love so many of the teachings of Jesus, but there are some things He said that trouble me. They almost sound as if I have to earn my salvation. Are all of His teachings for us today?

O F ALL THE disturbing aspects of the hyper-grace message, perhaps the most alarming is its claim that almost all of the teachings of Jesus are not for us today—that they are old covenant, not new. The fact is, as the Lord's sheep we should love His words more than life itself. Jesus is our Good Shepherd (John 10:11) and our Great Shepherd (Heb. 13:20), and He said His sheep hear His voice (John 10:27). We hear His voice most clearly in His words.

Jesus said that His words were spirit and life (John 6:63), and that if we remained in Him and His words remained in us, we could ask Him for whatever we desired and it would be given to us (John 15:7). That's why when He instructed His disciples to go into all the world and make disciples of the nations, He told them they were to teach these new disciples to obey His words. As stated in Matthew 28:19–20, "Go therefore and make disciples of all nations, baptizing them in the name of the Father and of the Son and of the Holy Spirit, *teaching them to observe all things I have commanded you.* And remember, I am with you always, even to the end of the age" (emphasis added).

Jesus even said that if we love Him, we will keep His commandments (John 14:15), explaining, "He who has My commandments and keeps them is the one who loves Me. And he who loves Me will be loved by My Father. And I will love him and will reveal Myself to him" (John 14:21). His commandments bring life, not death, and we find His commandments in His words.

Read the following wonderful words from our Master and ask yourself, "Do these apply to me as one of His followers, or were they meant just for the Jewish crowds who heard Him teach two thousand years ago?"

- "I am the bread of life. Whoever comes to Me shall never hunger, and whoever believes in Me shall never thirst" (John 6:35).

- "I am the light of the world. Whoever follows Me shall not walk in the darkness, but shall have the light of life" (John 8:12).

- "I am the door. If anyone enters through Me, he will be saved and will go in and out and find pasture" (John 10:9).

- "I am the good shepherd. The good shepherd lays down His life for the sheep" (John 10:11). "I am the good shepherd. I know My sheep and am known by My own" (v. 14).

- "I am the resurrection and the life. He who believes in Me, though he may die, yet shall he live. And whoever lives and believes in Me shall never die" (John 11:25–26).

- "I am the way, the truth, and the life. No one comes to the Father except through Me" (John 14:6).

- "I am the vine, you are the branches. He who remains in Me, and I in

him, bears much fruit. For without
Me you can do nothing" (John 15:5).

Thank You, Jesus, for these wonderful words!
Of course they apply to us today—every word,
every syllable, and every letter.

How about these sayings of Jesus? Do they
apply to us today as well?

- "Ask and it will be given to you; seek
  and you will find; knock and it will
  be opened to you. For everyone
  who asks receives, and he who
  seeks finds, and to him who knocks,
  it will be opened" (Matt. 7:7–8).

- "Come to Me, all you who labor and
  are heavily burdened, and I will
  give you rest. Take My yoke upon
  you, and learn from Me. For I am
  meek and lowly in heart, and you
  will find rest for your souls. For My
  yoke is easy, and My burden is light"
  (Matt. 11:28–30).

- "Look, I give you authority to
  trample on serpents and scor-
  pions, and over all the power of the
  enemy. And nothing shall by any
  means hurt you. Nevertheless do
  not rejoice that the spirits are subject to you, but rather rejoice that
  your names are written in heaven"
  (Luke 10:19–20).

How about the parable of the prodigal son,
where the father comes running to meet his
wayward son as he makes his way back home
(Luke 15:11–32)? How about the parable of
the Pharisee and the tax collector, where the
former is rebuked for his religious pride and
the latter is commended for recognizing his
need for mercy (Luke 18:9–14)? How about the
parables of the treasure hidden in the field and
the pearl of great price, which say that the dis-
covery of Jesus is so wonderful that we must
joyfully leave everything else behind to follow
Him (Matt. 13:44–46)?

Aren't all of these incredible, life-giving, life-changing, precious words from our Savior, words to be embraced rather than rejected? Is it any wonder, then, that Jesus said heaven and earth would pass away but His words would never pass away (Matt. 24:35)? And is it any wonder that He told His apostles shortly before He died that afterward, when they received the Holy Spirit, the Spirit would bring His words back to their remembrance (John 14:26)? Thank God that the Spirit did bring Jesus's words back to their remembrance so they could preserve these words for us today. Where would we be without the words of Jesus?

WE LEARN ABOUT JESUS
THROUGH HIS WORDS

It's great to point to the Cross and to extol everything Jesus did for our salvation—is there any subject more glorious than this?—and we should preach on the death and resurrection of Jesus day and night. But that is only the beginning. We are called to have an intimate relationship with Jesus, and we cannot have that relationship in full without knowing who He is and what He says. And like any other relationship, *we learn about Him through His words.*

Jesus spoke these amazing words to His disciples in John 15: "Greater love has no man than this: that a man lay down his life for his friends. You are My friends if you do whatever I command you. I no longer call you servants, for a servant does not know what his master does. But I have called you friends, for everything that I have heard from My Father have I made known to you" (vv. 13–15).

Did Jesus say this only to His Jewish followers then, or does this apply to all of us today? Does He call you and me His friends? Yes, He does! How do we know this? We know this through His words. And as His friends we understand what pleases Him, what He requires, and what He promises through His words. Can you really have a close relationship with anyone as a friend while ignoring that person's words?

Unfortunately some modern grace teachers claim that the words Jesus spoke before the Cross were exclusively for the Jewish audience that heard Him at that time, claiming that it is only those few recorded words Jesus spoke after the Cross—once He was resurrected—that apply to us today. Nothing could be further from the truth.

Of course, like the rest of the Bible, we need to interpret everything in its proper context. To give one example, all of us agree that Paul's letters to Timothy were not just for Timothy but are for us as well. At the same time, we recognize that Timothy was a young church leader, and not all of us are young and not all of us are church leaders. So all of us learn from verses like 1 Timothy 4:12–13 (where Paul instructs Timothy not to let anyone despise his youth and then gives him an exhortation to carry out his leadership role decisively), but they don't apply as directly to every reader as they would apply to a young church leader like Timothy.

In the same way, in 2 Timothy 4:13, when Paul asked Timothy to bring him his cloak, his books, and his parchments, it's clear that this does not apply to us directly—Paul died more than 1,950 years ago, and his cloak, books, and parchments are obviously nowhere to be found—yet none of us would therefore say, "Second Timothy is not for the church today!" Of course not.

It's the exact same thing with the words of Jesus. Some of His words had specific application to a certain audience at a certain time, such as His severe rebukes of the hypocritical religious leaders, whom He condemned to hell (Matt. 23). Not only is this condemnation not for us as believers today (Rom. 8:1), but some of the specifics hardly apply to us either. (See, for example, Matthew 23:16–20, where Jesus rebukes the leaders for their hypocritical oaths sworn by the temple.) So when we read this chapter, we examine our own lives for hypocrisy, but we don't hear the Lord saying to us, "Woe to you, scribes and Pharisees, hypocrites!" (Matt. 23:13)—unless, of course, that's exactly who we are, in which case we need to come to the Lord in repentance, asking for salvation.

As for the words Jesus spoke to His disciples, those certainly apply to us, since that *is* exactly who we are and who we are called to be. (Note that in the Book of Acts, the followers of Jesus are most commonly called "disciples.") That means that the Sermon on the Mount, which was delivered first and foremost to Jesus's disciples (Matt. 5:1–2), applies directly to us.

"But that's what troubles me," you say. "Jesus said in the Sermon on the Mount that my righteousness has to exceed that of the religious teachers, that if my right hand causes me to sin I have to cut it off and throw it away, and that if someone asks me for anything, I'm supposed to give it to them, which theoretically could mean my house and my car and even my family. How can this apply to me? It certainly doesn't sound like grace."

These are great questions! It's as if Jesus tells us in one part of the Bible that all we need to do is believe Him and ask for mercy (see, for example, Luke 18:9–14 and John 3:16), while in other parts of the Bible He tells us that unless we give up everything, we can't be His disciples. I can see how this can seem confusing. On top of that, it seems that some of the things He calls for are impossible. Is there, then, something to be said for the argument that His teachings before the Cross don't apply to us today?

Let's first demolish the idea that Jesus came with an "Old Testament" message and that only after the Cross do we get the real "New Testament" message. As John explained, speaking of Jesus (and note the words I highlighted):

> The Word became flesh and dwelt among us, and we saw His glory, the glory as the only Son of the Father, full of *grace and truth*. John bore witness of Him and cried out, "This was He of whom I said, 'He who comes after me is preferred before me, for He was before me.'" We have all received from His fullness *grace upon grace*. For the law was

given through Moses; *grace and truth*
came through Jesus Christ.
—JOHN 1:14–17, EMPHASIS ADDED

Jesus is the very embodiment of the grace of
God, the Person through whom God's grace is
expressed, and even during His earthly ministry those who heard Him and believed in Him
received "grace upon grace." Not only so, but
in contrast with the Law, which came through
Moses, grace and truth came through Jesus.
How then can anyone possibly claim that the
words Jesus spoke are not part of the message
of grace?

In addition, Luke writes, "The law and the
prophets were in force until John; since then, *the
good news of the kingdom of God has been proclaimed*, and everyone is urged to enter it" (Luke
16:16, NET, emphasis added). So, the ministry
of John the Immerser marks the turning point,
and as he introduces Jesus as the Messiah, from
that point on, "the good news of the kingdom
of God has been proclaimed." That's how the
four Gospels got their name—the word *gospel*

means "good news," and that's why Jesus said to the people in one particular location, "I must preach *the good news of the kingdom of God* to the other towns as well; for I was sent for this purpose" (Luke 4:43, ESV).

Jesus preached the gospel, not the Law, and by preaching the gospel, He brought out the full meaning of the Law and the Prophets, pointed to the ultimate goal (Matt. 5:17–20; Luke 16:16–17). And that means that the words of Jesus are most certainly for us, His disciples, just as they were for His disciples when He traveled with them through ancient Israel.

WHAT ABOUT JESUS'S RADICAL TEACHINGS?

What about Jesus's radical calls to leave everything and follow Him? Do they still apply to us today? Of course they do! As we noted in chapter 7, Jesus requires everything from all of us, not to earn His favor or salvation but rather because of His favor and salvation. He died for us, and now we live for Him. As Paul wrote to the

Corinthians, "For the love of Christ constrains us, because we thus judge: that if one died for all, then all have died. And He died for all, that those who live should not from now on live for themselves, but for Him who died for them and rose again" (2 Cor. 5:14–15).

This is not a truth that beats us over the head in condemnation. It is one that calls and invites us. It is the Master saying to each of us, "Put away the lusts of this world and reject the gods of this age and give yourselves completely to Me." It is the Bridegroom saying to His bride, "Leave your other lovers and have Me alone as your heavenly Husband," just as every husband and wife who make a true marriage commitment say good-bye to other relationships, pledging themselves to each other alone. This is what love does, and this is how love responds.

So when I hear Jesus say, "Any of you who does not forsake all that he has cannot be My disciple" (Luke 14:33), I say in response, "I belong to You, Lord—heart, soul, mind, and strength. I'm all Yours!" And when I hear Him say, "If any man would come after Me, let him deny himself and take up his cross and follow Me" (Mark 8:34), I say, "Lord, by Your grace, I have renounced every claim to my own life and gladly take up my cross and follow You!" This is my response to His grace, my joyful sacrifice in answer to His, my giving my life for Him in return for Him giving His life for me.

This is not salvation by works; it is our heartfelt response to the Lord's amazing grace. Let's not confuse the two.

And if someone should say, "I choose not to take up my cross; salvation by grace is enough for me," I would say in response, "Then you are a stranger to salvation by grace."

What about the radical teachings of Jesus in the Sermon on the Mount? There He said things such as, "If your right eye causes you to sin, pluck it out and throw it away....And if your right hand causes you to sin, cut it off and throw it away. For it is profitable for you that one of your members should perish, and not that your whole body be thrown into hell" (Matt. 5:29–30).

Some hyper-grace teachers have said to me, "Because we take the words of Jesus so seriously, we know these don't apply to us. Does He actually mean we're supposed to cut off the offending member or pluck out the offending eye? Obviously not! This proves these words were just for His Jewish hearers before the Cross."

With no disrespect toward these teachers, I have to say to them in response, "Are you really serious with that answer? Really?"

First, are we to think that the Lord's Jewish hearers during His earthly ministry couldn't recognize a figure of speech and actually went around hacking off their hands and plucking out their eyes? There was a time when the Church of England felt it would be wrong for common people to have a version of the Bible they could understand, arguing that only clergy could understand passages like this. It was argued in response that people knew how to differentiate between literal and figurative language, and the proof is that out of the hundreds of millions of Christians who have read this passage, you'd be hard-pressed to find one person who actually took it literally.

Second, if the Sermon on the Mount (along with the other teachings Jesus gave) was just for those who heard Jesus speak before the Cross, then why did Matthew (along with the other Gospel authors) record these words for the church decades later? And why did the church prize them so, reading them on a regular basis in their gatherings?

Third, why single out the words of Jesus as not applying to us today, when we find meaning and application from the words of Isaiah and Jeremiah and the other prophets, not to mention the words of Psalms and Proverbs and some of the other Old Testament books? Why say that only Jesus's words don't apply to us today? That seems especially bizarre.

Fourth, it is true that in ourselves we cannot keep His commandments, but that's where grace comes in. God's grace forgives us our sins and shortcomings, saving us and making us children of God. And then God's grace empowers and enables us, giving us the ability to live in the Spirit and overcome the lusts and desires of the flesh.

So the teachings of Jesus, in and of themselves, were always impossible in the flesh, and that's what made His listeners call out to God for grace and help. That's what He provides us through His death and resurrection, and we, of all people, can now live out to the full what He requires. And when we fall short, that glorious grace is there to cleanse us afresh and to call us to obedience.

In short, we prize the words of Jesus our Savior, our King, and our Friend, drinking them in as spirit and life. And we interpret them in context as we interpret the rest of the Bible, applying to ourselves that which was meant for His followers. Then, by His amazing grace, we believe His promises and act on His commands. As a result, we are blessed—wonderfully, gloriously blessed.

We are also utterly immovable. As Jesus taught:

> Whoever hears these sayings of Mine, and does them, I will liken him to a wise man who built his house on the rock: and the rain descended, the floods came, and the winds blew and beat on that house; and it did not fall, for it was founded on the rock. But everyone who hears these sayings of Mine, and does not do them, will be like a foolish man who built his house on the sand: and the rain descended, the floods came, and the winds blew and beat on that house; and it fell. And great was its fall.
> —MATTHEW 7:24–27, NKJV

As God's beloved children we are not those who hear the Lord's words and do not obey them, thereby deceiving ourselves. Rather, we are those who hear, obey, and are blessed (Jacob [James] 1:22–25). That is our response to grace, and we accomplish it by grace.

Chapter 11

IS GOD ALWAYS PLEASED WITH US AS HIS CHILDREN?

I know I'm far from perfect, but if God sees me through Jesus, doesn't that mean He sees me as perfect? And does that mean I'm always pleasing to Him? When I feel God's favor, I'm so encouraged, but when I feel He's not happy with me, it's like the bottom falls out. How do I sort this out?

I F YOU WATCH modern grace teachers on TV or read their books, you may get the impression that God is always happy and always pleased with His children. In addition to teaching that we are made completely and totally holy the moment we are saved, modern grace teachers claim that God always sees us as perfect in His sight. And because we are always seen as perfectly righteous before God, there is nothing we can (or should) do to try to please Him (a concept we addressed in chapter 7). Is this true? Are we already totally pleasing in God's sight?

Again we see God's glorious truth being mixed with dangerous error. Because God is now our Father and we are His children, we have a personal relationship with Him. That means we can please Him or displease Him, just as in any other personal relationship. But His love for us is deeper than we could ever imagine, and His disposition toward us is to bless us and do good to us, not to destroy us or drive us away. And what Jesus did on the cross for us puts us in a special place before the Father. What this means is that we must seek to live lives that are pleasing to Him while also being absolutely secure in His love.

Before we discuss what the Word says about the potential of displeasing God, let's look at what the Word says about His disposition toward us. We saw previously that the Lord calls us His friends, beginning with God and Abraham in Isaiah 41:8 and continuing with Jesus and His disciples in John 15:13–15. Then, at the Last Supper on the night He was betrayed, Jesus said this to His disciples: "I have earnestly desired to eat this Passover with you before I suffer. For I tell you, I will never eat it again until it is fulfilled in the kingdom of God" (Luke 22:15–16).

This is absolutely remarkable. The Son of God, who enjoyed perfect fellowship with His Father in heaven before coming down to this earth, the One whom angels worship, the One who knew that those very disciples would abandon Him and betray Him in a matter of hours, that same Son of God earnestly desired to eat His last meal with the disciples before He suffered. They were

His best friends here on earth, and He wanted their company at this critical time immediately before He would lay His life down for them, His friends.

But what about their many failings? What about their immaturity? What about all the stupid things they had said and done over the previous few years? Only minutes after Jesus spoke those words just quoted, the disciples got into an argument about which of them was the greatest (Luke 22:24). How carnal could they be? Yet Jesus loved them so dearly, He really looked forward to sharing a last meal with them before He suffered. Their company at that moment meant everything to Him. And that reflects the Father's heart to us.

Let me give you an illustration. Almost twenty years ago there was a young man who was a student in the ministry school I led. He was born and raised outside the United States and was taught to show real respect toward his elders, and he always treated me with honor. At that time my ministry schedule was very intense, averaging as much as eighty to one hundred hours a week. (This was in the midst of a tremendous season of revival and outpouring, so my schedule was as glorious as it was intense.)

One day we were both at the airport at the same time and were about to eat at the same place. When I saw him, I invited him to join me for lunch, but he politely declined, and I felt sure I knew exactly why. In his mind I had no choice but to invite him to sit with me since it was just the two of us there and it would have seemed rude if I failed to do so. But he knew how heavy my schedule was and understood how much I needed time alone, so he assumed that I was merely being polite; hence he declined my invitation. I knew that's what he was thinking, so I said to him, "I would prefer it if you ate with me." He smiled again and sat down to eat with me.

You see, he needed to know that it was *my preference* to have a meal with him, and when he realized that, he was very happy to oblige. After he graduated from our school, he began to work on the staff of our school, and today, many years later, we are very good friends.

This reflects God's heart toward you if you are one of His children. His preference is to spend time with you. He enjoys when you go to Him in prayer and worship. He likes being in your company, although He may not like everything you do and although there may be times when you grieve Him. But like any good father, He loves to be with His children, and like any real friend, He enjoys spending time with His companions.

At times this can be hard to comprehend because we know our own shortcomings only too well, but it is true, and it is in keeping with the love of God. That's how good He is!

Our oldest granddaughter is fifteen, and when she was younger, if our families were just standing around and talking, she would come over to me and lean on me. I thought to myself, "She is so sweet. She knows that her grandpa really enjoys when she does this." Then I realized, "Actually she does it because she enjoys leaning on her big, strong grandpa!"

To say it again: God is not just doing what is mandatory by spending time with us when we come to Him in prayer and worship. He is not simply doing His duty. No, He loves us, and He eagerly desires true fellowship with us—as we talk to Him while driving our cars, as we share our deepest burdens and concerns in our private journals, as we weep over the loss of a loved one, and as we celebrate a miraculous victory in our lives. He enjoys being included in the adventure of our lives, and He wants us to be blessed, not cursed.

Look at His disposition toward Israel in the Old Testament:

> Who is a God like you, who pardons sin and forgives the transgression of the remnant of his inheritance? You do not stay angry forever but delight to show mercy. You will again have compassion on us; you will tread our sins underfoot and hurl all our iniquities into the depths of the sea.
>
> —MICAH 7:18–19, NIV

He will not always chide, nor will he
keep his anger forever. He does not deal
with us according to our sins, nor repay
us according to our iniquities. For as
high as the heavens are above the earth,
so great is his steadfast love toward
those who fear him; as far as the east
is from the west, so far does he remove
our transgressions from us. As a father
shows compassion to his children, so
the LORD shows compassion to those
who fear him. For he knows our frame;
he remembers that we are dust.
                    —PSALM 103:9–14, ESV

That is our heavenly Father, and all this was
expressed before the fullest revelation of His
love as seen in the Cross. In light of that sacrifi-
cial demonstration, Paul wrote:

While we were yet weak, in due time
Christ died for the ungodly. Rarely for a
righteous man will one die. Yet perhaps
for a good man some would even dare
to die. But God demonstrates His own
love toward us, in that while we were yet

sinners, Christ died for us. How much
more then, being now justified by His
blood, shall we be saved from wrath
through Him. For if while we were enemies, we were reconciled to God by
the death of His Son, how much more,
being reconciled, shall we be saved by
His life. Furthermore, we also rejoice
in God through our Lord Jesus Christ,
through whom we have now received
reconciliation.

—ROMANS 5:6–11

Meditate on these words, and let them sink
deep into your heart and your mind. Through
Jesus we have been reconciled to God, and
through Him we will be eternally saved.

GOD SEES US AS HIS BELOVED CHILDREN

That is how God sees us—not as perfect or
without fault, but as His beloved children, saved
forever by the blood of His Son and made into
something beautiful in and through Him. And
as His beloved children, we can bring Him joy

or grief. Otherwise, it is not a real relationship. And as His beloved children, we can do things that please Him or displease Him, as these New Testament verses make clear:

- "Find out what *pleases the Lord*" (Eph. 5:10, NIV, emphasis added).

- "So we make it our goal to *please him*" (2 Cor. 5:9, NIV, emphasis added).

- And we pray this "so that you may live a life worthy of the Lord and *please him in every way*: bearing fruit in every good work, growing in the knowledge of God" (Col. 1:10, NIV, emphasis added).

- "Brothers and sisters, we instructed you *how to live in order to please God*, as in fact you are living. Now we ask you and urge you in the Lord Jesus to do this more and more" (1 Thess. 4:1, NIV, emphasis added).

- "We are not trying *to please people but God*, who tests our hearts" (1 Thess. 2:4, NIV, emphasis added).

What does this mean on a practical level? Paul explains here:

> Walk in a manner worthy of the calling with which you were called. With all humility, meekness, and patience, bearing with one another in love, be eager to keep the unity of the Spirit in the bond of peace.
>
> —EPHESIANS 4:1–3

> Speaking the truth in love, we are to grow up in every way into him who is the head, into Christ.
>
> —EPHESIANS 4:15, ESV

> You must no longer walk as the Gentiles do, in the futility of their minds
>
> —EPHESIANS 4:17, ESV

> Therefore, putting away lying, let every man speak truthfully with his neighbor,

for we are members of one another. Be
angry but do not sin. Do not let the sun
go down on your anger. Do not give
place to the devil. Let him who steals
steal no more. Instead, let him labor,
working with his hands things which
are good, that he may have something
to share with him who is in need. Let
no unwholesome word proceed out
of your mouth, but only that which is
good for building up, that it may give
grace to the listeners. And do not
grieve the Holy Spirit of God, in whom
you are sealed for the day of redemption. Let all bitterness, wrath, anger,
outbursts, and blasphemies, with all
malice, be taken away from you. And
be kind one to another, tenderhearted,
forgiving one another, just as God in
Christ also forgave you.

—Ephesians 4:25–32

You say, "But I thought God saw me through
Jesus, in which case He doesn't see my shortcomings and sins but instead sees Jesus in all His

perfection." That's an interesting concept, but it's actually not taught anywhere in the Bible. Even less is it taught that God simply *sees us* as perfect. Quite the opposite, and it is Jesus Himself who tells us this in the Book of Revelation, where He brings specific messages to seven churches in Asia Minor, addressing the "angel" (or messenger or leader) of each congregation.

Note what He says at the beginning of each message: "I know your works" (Rev. 2:2, 19; 3:1, 8, 15); "I know your…tribulation and your poverty" (Rev. 2:9); "I know where you dwell" (Rev. 2:13, ESV). Then He begins to speak to each congregation, commending them for what He was pleased with (for example, He commends Ephesus, the first in the list, for their toil, perseverance, and faithfulness, and for exposing false apostles) and then rebuking them for what He was displeased with (in the case of Ephesus, it was for leaving their first love).

He didn't just say to them, "Because you are in Me, I only see you as perfect, and my Father only sees you as perfect." Not at all. He had strong words of correction for five out of the seven churches, calling them to repent or else. And in each case He closed with a word of encouragement and promise.

This might make you uncomfortable, but I'm quite sure those messages made the believers in those churches uncomfortable too. It was all an expression of the Lord's love for them—and it is a jealous, intense love for sure.

You might say, "But I heard a teaching that Jesus was only addressing the pastors of those churches; that's why His speech was unusually harsh." Yes, He was speaking to the angels (or pastors or leaders) of those churches, but that was on behalf of the people in each congregation. As the Lord says seven times in Revelation chapters 2 and 3, "He who has an ear, let him hear what the Spirit says *to the churches*"—not "to the leaders of the churches." Could He have made it any clearer? The leaders were to deliver the messages to the people. That's whom Jesus was ultimately addressing.

We can also see clearly that He was speaking to the people and not just each leader when He rebuked the whole congregation for their sin before singling out some congregants who were doing well, as in Sardis. To the congregation as a whole in Sardis, He said, "I know your works. You have the reputation of being alive, but you are dead. Wake up, and strengthen what remains and is about to die, for I have not found your works complete in the sight of my God. Remember, then, what you received and heard. Keep it, and repent. If you will not wake up, I will come like a thief, and you will not know at what hour I will come against you" (Rev 3:1–3, ESV). To the few who were not defiled in Sardis, He said, "You have a few names even in Sardis who have not soiled their garments. They shall walk with Me in white, for they are worthy" (Rev. 3:4).

We dare not trivialize or ignore these words, since Revelation ends with a warning not to add or take away from the words of this sacred book (Rev. 22:18–19)—and that certainly includes what

Jesus said in it. And if there is anything clear and applicable in Revelation, a book filled with mystery and wonder, it is these messages to the seven churches of Asia Minor, the lesson being that if the Lord rebuked His blood-bought people then, He will rebuke them today. And if He didn't see them as perfect back then, He won't see us as perfect today. To quote our Savior again, "Those whom I love, I rebuke and discipline. Therefore be zealous and repent" (Rev. 3:19).

Frankly, if anything exposes the error of the hyper-grace teachers, it's their attempt to downplay, reinterpret, or ignore the Lord's words in Revelation, words that were spoken decades after the Lord's death and resurrection, words that were spoken to His church. Why not embrace everything He had to say, drinking in His words as spirit and life (John 6:63; also see chapter 10, "Do the Words of Jesus Apply to Us Today?")? When you realize that God is absolutely committed to you; that He took the initiative to save you when you were a sinful rebel; that He gladly paid for your sins with the blood of His Son; that

He is extraordinarily long-suffering toward you and tender in heart; that He delights in showing you mercy; that He understands your frame; that He sees you as a forgiven, blood-washed saint, set apart to be holy; that He is for you, not against you; surely your only reaction can be, "Then I want to bring Him joy! I want to please Him with every fiber of my being!"

What happens when you fall short? You should turn back to Him at once, remembering that He is quick to forgive you and wash you clean, also understanding that His Spirit will make you uncomfortable in your sin but will not condemn you for your sin. This is what it means to have a real, intimate, personal relationship with God, a concept that other religions, like Islam, cannot possibly comprehend, since in their eyes God is too exalted to relate to His servants in this way.

How glorious it is, then, to have God as our Father and to have Jesus as our Friend. And how amazing it is to have fellowship with the Holy Spirit (2 Cor. 13:14). Because of this intimate relationship, Paul writes, "Do not grieve the Holy

Spirit of God, in whom you are sealed for the day of redemption" (Eph. 4:30).

We can grieve Him by sinning against one another, and we can grieve Him by sinning directly against Him. This is taught clearly throughout the entire New Testament, and rather than trying to change the Word to fit our theology, we should change our theology to fit the Word. It will do our souls well.

A. W. Tozer expressed things well:

> Always remember that God is easy to get along with, and if your heart is right, He is not too concerned about the formula. God is kind and good and gracious, because there are some of us that are just too hard to get along with. If God were as hard to get along with as we are, there would be one perpetual quarrel between our souls and God. God has to be easy to live with, and if He knows you mean right, He will let you make all sorts of mistakes and will not care.
>
> But just as soon as self gets in and you mean wrong, the holiest thing you

do is unholy. As soon as you curse your conduct with self or sin, everything you do becomes wrong. But as long as you love God and people, He lets you tumble around a lot and won't mind a bit and sits and watches you as a mother fox, lying in the sunshine with her chin on her paws, with a smile on her face and watches her little puppies. God knows that the most mature of us still need coddling sometimes, and so He is quick to overlook our ignorance, but He is never quick to overlook our sins.[1]

We should be thankful that God does not overlook our sins, since those sins can be deadly. Instead, He deals with us in His love, which also means discipline and correction. But as long as I know He is for me and not against me, and that everything He does is for my ultimate good, both in this world and in the world to come, I am confident, secure, and blessed. You can be too!

Chapter 12

IS IT POSSIBLE TO LOSE YOUR SALVATION?

If there's one thing that terrifies me, it's the idea that I could lose my salvation. It strikes me as being the exact opposite of grace, since it implies there's something we must do to stay saved.

As I've mentioned in previous chapters, the modern grace message would tell us that as believers we are perfectly righteous before God and nothing we do can ever change that. This suggests that once we are saved, nothing can change our standing before God—even willful, persistent sin. Scripture makes it clear that this thinking is completely untrue. (See, for instance, John 15:6; 1 Corinthians 15:2; 2 Timothy 2:12; and Hebrews 10:26.) But does that mean we cannot be secure in our salvation? Absolutely not!

Rather than asking if it is possible to "lose" your salvation, let's ask the question, "Is it possible for you to walk away from God? As a follower of Jesus, do you still have a free will? Can you still make choices? If so, can you choose to deny Jesus and choose a life of sin instead?"

When looked at from this angle, it should be obvious that the answer is, "Yes, I still have a free will, and I can still make choices as a believer, so theoretically it would be possible for me to deny the Lord and abandon Him."

You might say, "But I want to live for the Lord all the days of my life. I'm just afraid that I could mess up in some way and lose my salvation."

Well then, let's focus on that word *lose* for a moment. There's a reason I didn't want to use it.

You lose something accidentally, like losing your car keys, your glasses, or a business card. "Where did I put those keys? I can't find them anywhere."

That is not the way things are with God and salvation. You don't simply "lose" your salvation, as if it was as easy as that. God has promised to keep us, assuring us that nothing can separate us from His love (Rom. 8:31–39) and that no one can pluck us out of His hand (John 10:28–29). He is the author and the finisher of our faith (Heb. 12:2), and He who began a good work in us will see it through to completion (Phil. 1:6). He is our Savior; we do not save ourselves. And just as we didn't get saved by accident, we can't lose our salvation by accident.

This means that if you want to live for the Lord, you have nothing to worry about in terms of "losing" your salvation. He will keep you, help you, empower you, guide you, correct you, and deliver you until you see Him face-to-face. Think of it like being a passenger on a plane that is guaranteed to reach its destination overseas. Unless you choose to do something crazy and open the emergency door and jump, you will arrive at your destination safely.

It's the exact same thing with salvation. The "plane" you are flying in is piloted by a perfect pilot, and there is nothing that can bring this plane down—not enemy fire, not bad weather, not anything—and you can enjoy the ride without fear of crashing. If you choose to do something crazy and walk away from the Lord—in the case of the plane analogy, open the emergency door and jump—then you choose to forfeit your salvation. But as long as you want to reach your destination and stay on the plane, you have nothing whatsoever to worry about. In fact, you can even enjoy the ride!

You might say, "But that's what scares me. If I have any choice in the matter, then I could be lost forever." The fact is, you do have a choice. There is not a verse in the Bible that says that once we become believers, we do not have a free will in Jesus and are no longer capable of making spiritual choices. If that was the case, the entire New Testament would make no sense at all, since the Word constantly calls us to make choices *as believers*. But God has promised to keep you, so if you put your trust in Him rather than in yourself, you have nothing to worry about.

LET THE WORD SPEAK FOR ITSELF

You may be now thinking, "But the grace message makes me feel so much more secure, since it tells me that no matter what I do, no matter how many times I sin, even if I deny the Lord, He will not let me go."

Perhaps it makes you feel more secure, but what you're hearing is not true. That's what makes the message so dangerous: it exaggerates wonderful truths about God's love, kindness, and long-suffering and goes beyond what Scripture says. Why in the world would you want to take comfort by believing in something false? That would be like going to a doctor who says, "You are now cancer-free and that cancer will never come back," and then dying one year later from cancer. What kind of help is that?

Some say, "But once you have eternal life, it cannot be cut short. And once God makes you His child, you can't cease to be His child." But that's not what the Word says (which I will illustrate shortly), and I don't want to impose my theology on the Scriptures. Instead, I want to base my theology on the Scriptures, letting the Word speak for itself.

To repeat: Our Father has given us wonderful promises, and our salvation is not some flimsy thing that can be found one day and lost the next. Nor is our salvation dependent on our ability to "stay saved." It is God who is at work in us, and He will finish what He started. He will hear your cry for help, He will have mercy on you in your weakness, and He will forgive one hundred times a day if you come to Him for cleansing. But He will not keep you against your own will, which is

why the Lord gives us so many warnings in the
New Testament.

Consider just a few of the relevant passages:

> And you, who were formerly alienated
> and enemies in your mind by wicked
> works, yet now He has reconciled in
> the body of His flesh through death,
> to present you holy and blameless and
> above reproach in His sight, *if you con-*
> *tinue in the faith*, grounded and settled,
> and are not removed from the hope of
> the gospel, which you have heard, and
> which was preached to every creature
> which is under heaven, and of which I,
> Paul, have become a servant.
> —COLOSSIANS 1:21–23,
> EMPHASIS ADDED

> Therefore we should be more attentive
> to what we have heard, lest we drift
> away. For if the word spoken by angels
> was true, and every sin and disobedi-
> ence received a just recompense, how
> shall we escape if we neglect such a
> great salvation, which was first declared

by the Lord, and was confirmed to us by those who heard Him?

—HEBREWS 2:1–3

Be attentive, brothers, lest there be in any of you an evil, unbelieving heart, and you depart from the living God. But exhort one another daily, while it is called "Today," lest any of you be hardened through the deceitfulness of sin. For we have become partakers of Christ if we hold the beginning of our confidence firmly to the end, while it is said: "Today, if you will hear His voice, do not harden your hearts as in the rebellion."

—HEBREWS 3:12–15

For if after they have escaped the defilements of the world through the knowledge of the Lord and Savior Jesus Christ, and they are again entangled in them and are overcome, the latter end is worse for them than the beginning. For it would have been better for them not to have known the way of righteousness than to have known it and then turn back from the holy commandment that was delivered to them. But it has happened to them according to the true proverb, "The dog returns to his own vomit," and "the sow that was washed to her wallowing in the mud."

—2 PETER 2:20–22

The New Testament authors had no trouble issuing strong warnings to believers, sometimes putting these warnings side by side with God's glorious promises. Both are true, and both should be taken to heart. That's why Hebrews 12:2 can speak of Jesus as "the pioneer and perfecter of our faith" (NET) while Hebrews 12:25–29 can warn us about the dangers of refusing to obey God's voice. In the same way, Philippians 2:12–13 puts our responsibility side by side with God's responsibility, saying, "Therefore, my beloved, as you have always obeyed, not only in my presence, but so much more in my absence, work out your own salvation with fear and trembling. For God is the One working in you, both to will and to do His good pleasure."

To help put all this in perspective, let me give you some further background. Within evangelical circles there are three main beliefs concerning the possibility of a child of God forfeiting his or her salvation, and countless thousands of pages have been written debating the question. These are the three main views:

1. The teaching commonly known as "once saved, always saved" (OSAS) states that once you are truly saved, no matter how you live or what you do, even denying Jesus and turning your back on Him, you cannot lose your salvation. Although your sin might shorten your life or lessen your future rewards, you will still be eternally saved.

2. The teaching called the "perseverance of the saints" states that a true believer will not ultimately turn away from the Lord, and therefore if you claim to be born again and

die in sin, denying the Lord, you
were never truly saved.

3. The final teaching doesn't have
one specific name associated with
it, but it states that a true believer
can choose to apostasize, reject
God's grace, and forfeit salvation.
Although we are secure in Jesus, if
we ultimately reject Him, we forfeit
our secure standing.

Those holding to the first view point to verses
like Romans 8:38–39, which state that nothing
that can separate us from God's love, or John
10:26–29, which state that Jesus's sheep have
eternal life and no one can pluck them out of
His hand. Those holding to the second viewpoint
emphasize those same passages but also point
to verses such as 1 John 2:19, which states that
those who left the church were never really part
of it, or 1 John 3:6, which states that those who
continue to live in sin have never really known
the Lord. Those holding to the third viewpoint

look to verses such as Colossians 1:21–23, which state that our salvation is assured if we persevere in faith to the end, or 2 Peter 2:20–22, which state that it would be better never to have known the Lord than to know Him and then turn away from Him.

For the most part, hyper-grace teachers emphatically hold to the doctrine of "once saved, always saved" (viewpoint number 1), although some seem to hold to the doctrine of "perseverance of the saints" (viewpoint number 2), making comments such as, "It is totally impossible for a true Christian to reject Christ, since true Christians are one in spirit with Jesus. If someone claims to be a follower of Jesus and then denies Him and chooses a life of sin and rebellion, that person was never saved, no matter what they claim." (This is a paraphrase of some common hyper-grace teachings. You can find exact quotes in my book *Hyper-Grace*.)

Of course, there is an irony when modern grace teachers hold to views like this, since it ultimately puts the emphasis back on the believer's "performance." In other words, "If I claim to be a believer and I'm living right, then I'm saved; but if I claim to be a believer and have turned away from God, I guess I was never saved." This is obviously the last thing intended by my hyper-grace colleagues, but again, it is the logical conclusion to statements like the one just quoted.

How then do we sort things out? It's really very simple. *God's promises are to believers—to those who want to follow the Lord and whose lives belong to Him—not to rebels who have chosen sin and rejected His lordship.* Put another way, there is not a single promise anywhere in the Bible that God will bless us with eternal life if we ultimately reject Him and choose rebellion. We give people false assurance when we make that claim. (In other words, viewpoint number 1 is not true.)

Find me one verse anywhere in the Bible— just one—that gives assurance of eternal life and blessing to an unrepentant rebel who is living in willful, persistent sin, denying the

Lord in an ongoing, hardened way, and I will invite you to join me on national radio or TV and tell the whole world that I was wrong. Just one verse!

Without a doubt you'll find many verses promising mercy and forgiveness to those who turn back (thank God!), and you'll find many verses assuring us of God's keeping power, but note clearly that the promises are given to Jesus's sheep—to those who know His voice and follow Him (John 10:27)—rather than to those who reject His voice and walk away from Him. In short, viewpoints number 2 or 3 could be right, but number 1 cannot.

So, on a practical level, it comes down to this: if you have put your trust in the Lord and desire to serve Him, He has given you absolute assurance that He will never leave or forsake you, that He will keep you safe to the end, and that no one and nothing can separate you from His love. Rest secure in Him! He is the author and finisher of your faith!

But if you believe that since you were once saved, even if you reject Him and live in unrepentant sin you are still saved, then you have deceived yourself and are in danger of falling under God's judgment. (That's why Jesus and Paul often warned us not to be deceived; see, for example, Matthew 24:4–5 and 1 Corinthians 6:9–10.) If you walked away from the Lord, either you were never saved or you have forfeited your salvation, so turn back to Him now, knowing that He is quick to forgive, that He loves to show mercy, and that He can restore you to Himself with life, hope, and purpose through Jesus. To repeat: the promise of eternal life is only to Jesus's sheep, those who know His voice and follow Him.

But why would we ever want to walk away from Him? Everything we need is found in Him, and in Him alone is life—true, abundant life—so drink deeply of His incredible love. Be assured that He who began the good work in you will bring it to completion (Phil. 1:6). And if you find yourself playing games with sin and growing

213

distant from the Lord, get sober, get serious, and turn back to the Cross. The cleansing blood of Jesus will never lose its power.

NOTES

INTRODUCTION
AMAZING GRACE!

1. See my article "Recovering the Lost Letter of Jacob," CharismaNews.com, March 11, 2013, accessed January 19, 2016, http://www.charisma news.com/opinion/38591-recovering-the-lost -letter-of-jacob.

CHAPTER 1
IS GRACE A PERSON?

1. As cited in Michael L. Brown, *Go and Sin No More: A Call to Holiness* (Concord, NC: EqualTime Books, 1998, 2013), 205. Used by permission.

CHAPTER 2
ARE ALL OUR SINS—PAST, PRESENT, AND FUTURE—ALREADY FORGIVEN IN JESUS?

1. See Michael L. Brown, *Hyper-Grace* (Lake Mary, FL: Charisma House, 2014), 39–50.

CHAPTER 3
IF A BELIEVER FAILS TO CONFESS EVEN ONE SIN BEFORE HE DIES, WILL HE GO TO HELL?

1. Yoma 39a-b of the Babylonian Talmud can be read at Yashanet.com, accessed January 19, 2016, http://www.yashanet.com/library/temple /yoma39.htm.

CHAPTER 5
DOES GOD SEE US AS RIGHTEOUS?

1. Dr. Bob Gladstone, in communication with the author, June 7, 2013.
2. John H. Stoll, "Biblical Principles for Christian Maturity," LeadershipU, 1996, accessed January 19, 2016, http://www.leaderu.com/offices /stoll/maturity/chap20.html.

CHAPTER 6
WHAT DOES IT MEAN TO BE UNDER GRACE AND NOT THE LAW?

1. As quoted in Jason Meyer, *The End of the Law: Mosaic Covenant in Pauline Theology* (Nashville, TN: B&H Publishing, 2009), 2.

CHAPTER 8
ARE WE MADE COMPLETELY HOLY THE MOMENT WE ARE SAVED?

1. Clark Whitten, *Pure Grace: The Life Changing Power of Uncontaminated Grace*

(Shippensburg, PA: Destiny Image, 2012), 28.
See also Brown, *Hyper-Grace*, 8–21.

2.   J. Edwin Orr, *My All, His All* (Wheaton, IL:
Richard Owen Roberts Publishers, 1989), 7.

CHAPTER 11
IS GOD ALWAYS PLEASED WITH US AS HIS CHILDREN?

1.   A. W. Tozer, *And He Dwelt Among Us:
Teachings from the Gospel of John* (Ventura,
CA: Regal, 2009), 149–150.

Steps to Peace With God

1. God's Purpose: Peace and Life

God loves you and wants you to experience peace and life—abundant and eternal.

The Bible says ...

"We have peace with God through our Lord Jesus Christ." *Romans 5:1, NKJV*

"For God so loved the world that He gave His only begotten Son, that whoever believes in Him should not perish but have everlasting life." *John 3:16, NKJV*

"I have come that they may have life, and that they may have it more abundantly." *John 10:10, NKJV*

Since God planned for us to have peace and the abundant life right now, why are most people not having this experience?

2. Our Problem: Separation From God

God created us in His own image to have an abundant life. He did not make us as robots to automatically love and obey Him, but gave us a will and a freedom of choice.

We chose to disobey God and go our own willful way. We still make this choice today. This results in separation from God.

The Bible says ...

"For all have sinned and fall short of the glory of God." *Romans 3:23, NKJV*

"For the wages of sin is death, but the gift of God is eternal life in Christ Jesus our Lord." *Romans 6:23, NKJV*

Our choice results in separation from God.

Our Attempts

Through the ages, individuals have tried in many ways to bridge this gap ... without success ...

The Bible says ...

"There is a way that seems right to a man, but its end is the way of death."
Proverbs 14:12, NKJV

"But your iniquities have separated you from your God; and your sins have hidden His face from you, so that He will not hear."
Isaiah 59:2, NKJV

There is only one remedy for this problem of separation.

3. God's Remedy: The Cross

Jesus Christ is the only answer to this problem. He died on the cross and rose from the grave, paying the penalty for our sin and bridging the gap between God and people.

The Bible says ...

"For there is one God and one Mediator between God and men, the Man Christ Jesus."
1 Timothy 2:5, NKJV

"For Christ also suffered once for sins, the just for the unjust, that He might bring us to God."
1 Peter 3:18, NKJV

"But God shows his love for us in that while we were still sinners, Christ died for us." *Romans 5:8, ESV*

God has provided the only way ... we must make the choice ...

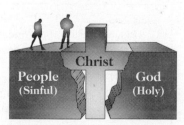

4. OUR RESPONSE: RECEIVE CHRIST

We must trust Jesus Christ and receive Him by personal invitation.

THE BIBLE SAYS ...

"Behold, I stand at the door and knock. If anyone hears My voice and opens the door, I will come in to him and dine with him, and he with Me." *Revelation 3:20, NKJV*

"But to all who did receive him, who believed in his name, he gave the right to become children of God." *John 1:12, ESV*

"If you confess with your mouth that Jesus is Lord and believe in your heart that God raised him from the dead, you will be saved." *Romans 10:9, ESV*

Are you here ... or here?

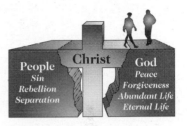

Is there any good reason why you cannot receive Jesus Christ right now?

HOW TO RECEIVE CHRIST:

1. Admit your need (say, "I am a sinner").
2. Be willing to turn from your sins (repent) and ask for God's forgiveness.
3. Believe that Jesus Christ died for you on the cross and rose from the grave.
4. Through prayer, invite Jesus Christ to come in and control your life through the Holy Spirit (receive Jesus as Lord and Savior).

WHAT TO PRAY:

Dear God,

    I know that I am a sinner. I want to turn from my sins, and I ask for Your forgiveness. I believe that Jesus Christ is Your Son. I believe He died for my sins and that You raised Him to life. I want Him to come into my heart and to take control of my life. I want to trust Jesus as my Savior and follow Him as my Lord from this day forward.

In Jesus' Name, amen.

_____   _____
Date   Signature

God's Assurance: His Word

If you prayed this prayer,

the Bible says …

"For 'everyone who calls on the name of the Lord will be saved.'"
Romans 10:13, ESV

Did you sincerely ask Jesus Christ to come into your life?
Where is He right now? What has He given you?

"For by grace you have been saved through faith. And this is not your own doing; it is the gift of God, not a result of works, so that no one may boast." *Ephesians 2:8–9, ESV*

the Bible says …

"He who has the Son has life; he who does not have the Son of God does not have life. These things I have written to you who believe in the name of the Son of God, that you may know that you have eternal life, and that you may continue to believe in the name of the Son of God."
1 John 5:12–13, NKJV

Receiving Christ, we are born into God's family through the supernatural work of the Holy Spirit, who indwells every believer. This is called regeneration or the "new birth."

This is just the beginning of a wonderful new life in Christ. To deepen this relationship you should:

1. Read your Bible every day to know Christ better.
2. Talk to God in prayer every day.
3. Tell others about Christ.
4. Worship, fellowship, and serve with other Christians in a church where Christ is preached.
5. As Christ's representative in a needy world, demonstrate your new life by your love and concern for others.

God bless you as you do.

Franklin Graham

If you want further help in the decision you have made, write to:
Billy Graham Evangelistic Association
1 Billy Graham Parkway, Charlotte, NC 28201-0001

1-877-2GRAHAM (1-877-247-2426)
BillyGraham.org/commitment

KT

Reading Group Choices

Selections for Lively Book Discussions

Paz & Associates

2005

For further information, contact:
Mark Kaufman, Editor
Reading Group Choices

Paz & Associates
1417 Sadler Rd. — PMB 274
Fernandina Beach, FL 32034-4466
800/260-8605 — phone
mkaufman@pazbookbiz.com — email

Visit our websites at:
www.readinggroupchoices.com
www.pazbookbiz.com

ISBN 0-9759742-0-3

We wish to thank the authors, agents, publicists, and our publishing colleagues who have continued to support this publication by calling to our attention some quality books for group discussion:

Algonquin Books
Downtown Press
HarperCollins
In One Press
Middleway Press
Oaklea Press
Platinum One Publishing
Red Wheel/Weiser/Conari
Silent River Press
Time Warner Book Group
Warwick & Associates
Yale University Press

Ballantine Books (Random House)
Grove/Atlantic
Hyperion Books
Louisiana State University Press
W.W. Norton
Penguin/Putnam Group
Plume Books
Rusoff Literary Agency
Silver Light Publishing
Vintage Books (Random House)
Windstream Publishing